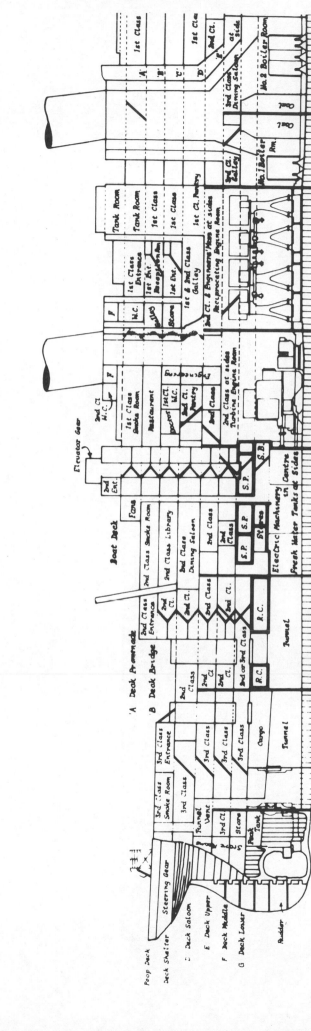

S.S. TITANIC

R.C. = Refrigerated Cargo
S.P. = Ships Provisions
S.B. = Switchboard

REPORT ON THE LOSS OF THE S.S.

TITANIC

REPORT ON THE LOSS OF THE S.S. TITANIC

ST MARTIN'S PRESS · NEW YORK

First published in the USA in 1990 by St Martin's Press
Scholarly and Reference Division
175 Fifth Avenue, New York, N.Y. 10010

Reprinted 1998

Library of Congress Cataloging-in-Publication-Data
Report on the loss of SS Titanic: report of a formal investigation into the circumstances attending the foundering on 15th April, 1912, of the British Steamship Titanic, of Liverpool, after striking ice in or near latitude 41° 46'N., logitude 50° 14'W., North Atlantic Ocean, whereby loss of life ensued.
    p. cm.
    "Presented to both Houses of Parliament by Command of His Majesty."
    Reprint. Originally published: 1912.
    1. T itanic (Steamship)   2. Shipwrecks—North Atlantic Ocean.
    ISBN 0 312 21487 1
I. Great Britain. Parliament.
VK1255.T6R47   1990   89-77159
368.12'3—dc20   CIP

Printed in Great Britain by
WBC Limited, Bridgend, Mid-Glamorgan.

INTRODUCTION

Such a biting cold air poured into my stateroom that I could not sleep, and the air had so strange an odor, as if it came from a clammy cave. I had noticed that same odor in the ice cave on the Eiger glacier. It all came back to me so vividly that I could not sleep, but lay in my berth until the cabin grew so very cold that I got up and turned on my electric stove. It threw a cheerful red glow around, and the room was soon comfortable; but I lay waiting. I have always loved both day and night on shipboard, and am never fearful of anything, but now I was nervous about the icy air.

Suddenly a queer quivering ran under me, apparently the whole length of the ship. Startled by the very strangeness of the shivering motion, I sprang to the floor. With too perfect a trust in that mighty vessel I again lay down. Someone knocked at my door, and the voice of a friend said: 'Come quickly to my cabin; an iceberg has just passed our window; I know we have just struck one.'

No confusion, no noise of any kind, one could believe no danger imminent. Our stewardess came and said she could learn nothing. Looking out into the companionway I saw heads appearing asking questions from half-closed doors. All sepulchrally still, no excitement. I sat down again. My friend was by this time dressed; still her daughter and I talked on, Margaret pretending to eat a sandwich. Her hand shook so that the bread kept parting company from the chicken. Then I saw she was frightened, and for the first time I was too, but why get dressed, as no one had given the slightest hint of any possible danger? An officer's cap passed the door. I asked: 'Is there an accident or danger of any kind?' 'None, so far as I know,' was his courteous answer, spoken quietly and most kindly. This same officer then entered a cabin a little distance down the companionway and, by this time distrustful of everything, I listened intently, and distinctly heard, 'We can keep the water out for a while.' Then, and not until then, did I realize the horror of an accident at sea. Now it was too late to dress; no time for a waist, but a coat and skirt were soon on; slippers were quicker than shoes; the stewardess put on our life-preservers, and we were just ready when Mr. Roebling came to tell us he would take us to our friend's mother, who was waiting above.

We passed by the palm room, where two short hours before we had listened to a beautiful concert, just as one might sit in one's own home. With never a realizing sense of being on the ocean, why should not one forget? – no motion, no noise of machinery, nothing suggestive of a ship. Happy, laughing men and women constantly passing up and down those broad, strong staircases, and the music went on and the ship went on – nearer and nearer to its end. So short a life, so horrible a death for that great, great ship. What is a more stupendous work than a ship! The almost human pieces of machinery, yet a helpless child, powerless in its struggle with an almighty sea, and the great boat sank, fragile as a rowboat.

How different are these staircases now! No laughing throng, but on either side stand quietly, bravely, the stewards, all equipped with the white, ghostly life-preservers. Always the thing one tries not to see even crossing a ferry. Now only pale faces, each form strapped about with those white bars. So gruesome a scene. We passed on. The awful good-byes. The quiet look of hope in the brave men's eyes as the wives were put into the lifeboats. Nothing escaped one at this fearful moment. We left from the Sun Deck, seventy-five feet above the water. Mr. Case and Mr. Roebling, brave American men, saw us to the lifeboat, made no effort to save themselves, but stepped back on deck. Later they went to an honored grave.

Our lifeboat, with thirty-six in it, began lowering to the sea. This was done amid the greatest confusion. Rough seamen all giving different orders. No officer aboard.

As only one side of the ropes worked, the lifeboat at one time was in such a position that it seemed we must capsize in mid-air. At last the ropes worked together, and we drew nearer and nearer the black, oily water. The first touch of our lifeboat on that black sea came to me as a last good-bye to life, and so we put off – a tiny boat on a great sea – rowed away from what had been a safe home for five days. The first wish on the part of all was to stay near the *Titanic*. We all felt so much safer near the ship. Surely such a vessel could not sink. I thought the danger must be exaggerated, and we could all be taken aboard again. But surely the outline of that great, good ship was growing less. The bow of the boat was getting black. Light after light was disappearing, and now those rough seamen put to their oars and we were told to hunt under seats, any place, anywhere, for a lantern, a light of any kind. Every place was empty. There was no water – no stimulant of any kind. Not a biscuit – nothing to keep us alive had we drifted long. Had not good *Carpathia*, with its splendid Captain Rostron, its orderly crew, come to our rescue we must have all perished. Our men knew nothing about the position of the stars, hardly how to pull together. Two oars were soon overboard. The men's hands were too cold to hold on. We stopped while they beat their hands and arms, then started on again. A sea, calm as a pond, kept our boat steady, and now that mammoth ship is fast, fast disappearing. Only one tiny light is left – a powerless little spark, a lantern fastened to the mast. Fascinated, I watched that black outline until the end. Then across the water swept that awful wail, the cry of those drowning people. In my ears I heard: 'She's gone, lads; row like hell or we'll get the devil of a swell.' And the horror, the helpless horror, the worst of all – need it have been?

This account by Miss Elizabeth W. Shutes portrays vividly the atmosphere among the first-class passengers on board the S.S. *Titanic* on that fateful night of 14 April 1912. The attempt to resolve her final question resulted in the enquiries held on both sides of the Atlantic, where surviving crew and passengers were questioned in the spring and summer of 1912. The two reports which followed, the British *Report on the Loss of the "Titanic" (S.S.)* and the American *Titanic Disaster, Report of the U.S. Committee on Commerce* sought to enquire into the nature of the disaster, its causes, and the adequacy of the safety procedures.

The task of preparing the clear, detailed and factual account which is reprinted here involved elucidating from survivors information which was naturally confused and conflicting or even altered with hindsight. This is well illustrated by the comments of Lord Mersey, the Wreck Commissioner, on the numbers saved by the lifeboats, which are recorded on p. 39 of the report: 'There was a tendency in the evidence to exaggerate the proportion of women to men and to diminish the number of crew.' He goes on, 'I do not attribute this to any wish on the part of the witnesses to mislead the Court, but to a natural desire to make the best case for themselves and their ship.' Obtaining a clear view of the course of events leading up to the disaster and of the activities immediately succeeding it was obviously not easy, given such circumstances.

Perhaps similar sentiments to those indicated by Lord Mersey also affected the memory of the incidents recorded on p. 40 of the report, in the section entitled, 'Conduct of Sir C. Duff Gordon and Mr. Ismay'. The report here describes as 'unfounded' 'the very gross charge against Sir Cosmo Duff Gordon that, having got into No. 1 boat he bribed the men in it to row away from drowning people.' This charge had been made in newspapers soon after the shipwreck and was discussed at some length in the subsequent enquiries. The records recall the account of Charles Hendricksen, a fireman who was one of the twelve rescued in No. 1 lifeboat:

When the ship sank we picked up nobody. The passengers would not listen to our going back. Of the twelve in the boat, seven were of the crew. Symons, who was in charge, said nothing and we all kept our mouths shut. None of the crew objected to going back. It was a woman who objected, Lady Duff Gordon, who said we would be swamped. People screaming for help could be heard by everyone in our boat. I suggested going back. Heard no one else do so. Mr. Duff Gordon upheld his wife.

After we got on the *Carpathia* Gordon sent for them all and said he would make then a present. He was surprised to receive five pounds from him the day after docking in New York.

Another fireman, R.W. Pusey, recounted:

> After the ship went down we heard cries for a quarter of an hour, or twenty minutes. Did not go back in the direction the *Titanic* had sunk. I heard one of the men say: 'We have lost our kit,' and then someone said: 'Never mind, we will give you enough to get a new kit.' I was surprised that no one suggested going back. I was surprised that I did not do so, but we were all half dazed. It does occur to me now that we might have gone back and rescued some of the strugglers. I heard Lady Duff Gordon say to Miss Francatelli: 'You have lost your beautiful nightdress,' and I said: 'Never mind, you have saved your lives; but we have lost our kit;' and then Sir Cosmo offered to provide us with new ones.

The charge against Sir Cosmo Duff Gordon was summed up at the British enquiry by Mr. A. Clement Edwards, MP, Counsel for the Dock Workers' Union:

> Here was a boat only a short distance from the ship, so near that the cries of those struggling in the water could be heard. Symons had been told to stand by the ship, and that imposed upon him a specific duty. It was shown in Hendricksen's evidence that there was to the fullest knowledge of those in the boat a large number of people in the water, and that someone suggested that they should return and try to rescue them. Then it was proved that one of the ladies, who was shown to be Lady Duff Gordon, had said that the boat might be swamped if they went back, and Sir Cosmo Duff Gordon had admitted that this also represented his mental attitude at the time. He (Mr. Edwards) was going to say, and to say quite fearlessly, that a state of mind which could, while within the hearing of the screams of drowning people, think of so material a matter as the giving of money to replace kits was a state of mind which must have contemplated the fact that there was a possibility of rescuing some of these people, and the danger which might arise if this were attempted.
>
> He was not going to say that there was a blunt, crude bargain, or a deal done with these men: 'If you will not go back I will give you five pounds;' but he was going to suggest as a right and true inference that the money was mentioned at that time under these circumstances to give such a sense of ascendancy or supremacy to Sir Cosmo Duff Gordon in the boat that the view to which he gave expression that they should not go back would weigh more with the men than if he had given it as a piece of good advice. There were twenty-eight places on that boat and no one on board had a right to save his own life by avoiding any possible risk involved in filling the vacant places. To say the least of it, it was most reprehensible that there should have been any offer of money calculated to influence the minds of the men or to seduce them from their duty.

The events surrounding the rescue of Mr. Bruce Ismay, Managing Director of the White Star Line, which owned the *Titanic*, were likewise controversial (report, p. 40), and again it was Mr. Edwards who outlined the charge at the British enquiry. In doing so, he evinced a clear indication of the attitude of the Court in Lord Mersey's denial of the relevance of moral duty to the enquiry and thus the report:

> Coming to Mr. Ismay's conduct, Mr. Edwards said it was clear that that gentleman had taken upon himself to assist in getting women and children into the boats. He had also admitted that when he left the *Titanic* he knew she was doomed, that there were hundreds of people in the ship, that he didn't know whether or not there were any women or children left, and that he did not even go to the other side of the Boat Deck to see whether there were any women and children waiting to go. Counsel submitted that a gentleman occupying the position of managing director of the company owning the *Titanic*, and who had taken upon himself the duty of assisting at the boats, had certain special and further duties beyond an ordinary passenger's duties, and that he had no more right to save his life at the expense of any single person on board that ship than the captain would have had. He (Mr. Edwards) said emphatically that Mr. Ismay did not discharge his duty at that particular moment by taking a careless glance around the starboard side of the Boat Deck. He was one of the few persons who at the time had been placed in a position of positive

knowledge that the vessel was doomed, and it was his clear duty, under the circumstances, to see that someone made a search for passengers in other places than in the immediate vicinity of the Boat Deck.

Lord Mersey: Moral duty to you mean?

Mr. Edwards: I agree; but I say that a managing director going on board a liner, commercially responsible for it and taking upon himself certain functions, had a special moral obligation and duty more than is possessed by one passenger to another passenger.

Lord Mersey: But how is a moral duty relative to this enquiry? It might be argued that there was a moral duty for every man on board that every woman should take precedence, and I might have to inquire whether every passenger carried out his moral duty.

Controversy likewise remains unresolved regarding the safety measures provided for third-class passengers aboard the *Titanic*. The report categorically denies any preferential treatment given to first- and second-class passengers in boarding the lifeboats (pp. 40–1, 70). The table on p. 42 indicates why such a denial was necessary – 62·46 per cent of the 325 first-class passengers survived, in contrast to 37·94 per cent of the 1,316 third-class passengers, while, of the women in the first-class accommodation, 97·22 per cent were saved, as opposed to the 46·06 per cent of those in the third-class, and of the children, all those travelling first- and second-class were saved, while 65·38 per cent of those travelling third-class were killed. The report cites 'the difficulty in getting them [third-class passengers] up from their quarters, which were at the extreme ends of the ship' as a reason for the disproportion, though, by answering, 'No', to the question, 'Was the construction of the vessel and its arrangements such as to make it difficult for any class of passenger . . . to take full advantage of any of the existing provisions for safety?' (p. 71), sufficient room is left for doubt.

The detached viewpoint of the report clearly does not detract from the human drama of its concern. This is apparent from the very start of the account, where we read of the tragic failure of the Marconi operator, who was too busy transmitting passengers' messages to take sufficient notice of warnings of ice in the vicinity. The involvement in the disaster of the S.S. *Californian*, one of the ships sending warnings, is dealt with in section five of the report. The indictment of Captain Stanley Lord, who was in charge of the liner, for not rescuing survivors has been contested by those who claim that the lights on the horizon seen by passengers aboard the sinking *Titanic* were not those of the *Californian*, but those of a Norwegian vessel, the *Samson*, illegally hunting for seals in the area. Whatever the truth may be in this matter, what is disputed by none is the exemplary behaviour of Captain Arthur Rostron and his crew aboard the *Carpathia*, which arrived to pick up survivors on the dawn of April 15. In his testimony before the American enquiry, he recalled:

We picked up the first boat, which was in charge of an officer who I saw was not under full control of his boat. He sang out that he had only one seaman in the boat, so I had to manoeuvre the ship to get as close to the boat as possible, as I knew well it could be difficult to do the pulling. By the time we had the first boat's people it was breaking day, and then I could see the remaining boats all around within an area of about four miles. I also saw icebergs all around me. There were about twenty icebergs that would be anywhere from about 150 to 200 feet high, and numerous smaller bergs; also numerous ones we call 'growlers' anywhere from 10 to 12 feet high and 10 to 15 feet long, above the water.

Three first-hand accounts, revealing the full context of the report on this most famous of maritime disasters, conclude this brief introduction. The first is by Mrs. J.J. Brown of Denver, Colorado, whose personal communication to another American first-class passenger, Colonel Archibald Gracie, is recounted by him:

Instead of retiring to slumber, Mrs. Brown was absorbed in reading and gave little thought to the crash at her window overhead which threw her to the floor. Picking herself up she proceeded to see what the steamer had struck; but thinking nothing serious had occurred, though realizing that the engines had stopped immediately after the crash and the boat was at a standstill, she picked up her book and began reading again. Finally she saw her curtains moving while she was reading, but no one was visible. She again looked out and saw a man whose face was blanched, his eyes protruding, wearing the look of a haunted creature. He was gasping for breath and in an undertone gasped, 'Get your life-preserver.' He was one of the buyers for Gimbel Bros., of Paris and New York.

She got down her life-preserver, snatched up her furs and hurriedly mounted the stairs to A Deck, where she found passengers putting on life-belts like hers. Mrs. Bucknell approached and whispered, 'Didn't I tell you something was going to happen?' She found the lifeboats lowered from the falls and made flush with the deck. Madame de Villiers appeared from below in a nightdress and evening slippers, with no stockings. She wore a long woollen motorcoat. Touching Mrs. Brown's arm, in a terrified voice she said she was going below for her money and valuables. After much persuasion Mrs. Brown prevailed upon her not to do so, but to get into the boat. She hesitated and became very much excited, but was finally prevailed upon to enter the lifeboat. Mrs. Brown was walking away, eager to see what was being done elsewhere. Suddenly she saw a shadow and a few seconds later someone seized her, saying: 'You are going, too,' and she was dropped fully four feet into the lowering lifeboat. There was but one man in charge of the boat. As it was lowered by jerks by an officer above, she discovered that a great gush of water was spouting through the porthole from D Deck, and the lifeboat was in grave danger of being submerged. She immediately grasped an oar and held the lifeboat away from the ship.

When the sea was reached, smooth as glass, she looked up and saw the benign, resigned countenance, the venerable white hair and the Chesterfieldian bearing of the beloved Captain Smith with whom she had crossed twice before, and only three months previous on the *Olympic*. He peered down upon those in the boat, like a solicitous father, and directed them to row to the light in the distance – all boats keeping together.

Because of the fewness of men in the boat she found it necessary for someone to bend to the oars. She placed her oar in an oarlock and asked a young woman nearby to hold one while she placed the other on the further side. To Mrs. Brown's surprise, the young lady immediately began to row like a galley slave, every stroke counting. Together they managed to pull away from the steamer.

By this time E and C Decks were completely submerged. Those ladies who had husbands, sons or fathers on the doomed steamer buried their heads on the shoulders of those near them and moaned and groaned. Mrs. Brown's eyes were glued on the fast-disappearing ship. Suddenly there was a rift in the water, the sea opened up and the surface foamed like giant arms and spread around the ship and the vessel disappeared from sight, and not a sound was heard.

The second account comes from an article written for the *Semi-Monthly Magazine* of May 1912 by Mrs. Charlotte Collyer, a third-class passenger, who was rescued on lifeboat No. 14:

A little further on we saw a floating door that must have been torn loose when the ship went down. Lying upon it, face downward, was a small Japanese. He had lashed himself with a rope to his frail raft, using the broken hinges to make the knots secure. As far as we could see, he was dead. The sea washed over him every time the door bobbed up and down, and he was frozen stiff. He did not answer when he was hailed, and the officer hesitated about trying to save him.

'What's the use?' said Mr. Lowe. 'He's dead, likely, and if he isn't there's others better worth saving than a Jap!'

He had actually turned our boat around, but he changed his mind and went back. The Japanese was hauled on board, and one of the women rubbed his chest, while others chafed his hands and feet. In less time than it takes to tell, he opened his eyes. He spoke to us in his own tongue; then, seeing that we did not understand, he struggled to his feet, stretched his arms above his head, stamped his feet and in five minutes or so had almost recovered his strength. One of the sailors near to him was so tired that he could hardly pull his oar. The Japanese bustled over, pushed him from his seat, took his oar and worked like a hero until we were finally picked up. I saw Mr. Lowe watching him in open-mouthed surprise.

'By Jove!' muttered the officer, 'I'm ashamed of what I said about the little blighter. I'd save the likes o' him six times over if I got the chance.'

Finally, here is the account given by Colonel Gracie in his *The Truth about the Titanic*, first published in 1913, of the dramatic rescue attempt made by him and his friend, James Clinch Smith, from the sinking ship:

I was now working with the crew at the davits on the starboard side forward, adjusting them, ready for lowering the Engelhardt boat from the roof of the officers' house to the Boat Deck below. Some one of the crew on the roof, where it was, sang out, 'Has any passenger a knife?' I took mine out of my pocket and tossed it to him, saying, 'Here is a small penknife, if that will do any good.' It appeared to me then that there was more trouble than there ought to have been in removing the canvas cover and cutting the boat loose, and that some means should have been available for doing this without any delay. Meantime, four or five long oars were placed aslant against the walls of the officers' house to break the fall of the boat, which was pushed from the roof and slipped with a crash down on the Boat Deck, smashing several of the oars. Clinch Smith and I scurried out of the way and stood leaning with our backs against the rail, watching this procedure and feeling anxious lest the boat might have been stove in, or otherwise injured so as to cause her to leak in the water. The account of the junior Marconi operator, Harold S. Bride, supplements mine. 'I saw a collapsible boat,' he said, 'near a funnel, and went over to it. Twelve men were trying to boost it down to the Boat Deck. They were having an awful time. It was the last boat left. I looked at it longingly a few minutes; then I gave a hand and over she went.'

About this time I recall that an officer on the roof of the house called down to the crew at this quarter, 'Are there any seamen down there among you?' 'Aye, aye, sir,' was the response, and quite a number left the Boat Deck to assist in what I supposed to have been the cutting loose of the other Engelhardt boat up there on the roof. Again I heard an inquiry for another knife. I thought I recognized the voice of the second officer working up there with the crew. Lightoller has told me, and has written me as well, that 'boat A on the starboard side did not leave the ship,' while 'B was thrown down to the Boat Deck,' and was the one on which he and I eventually climbed. The crew had thrown the Engelhardt boat to the deck, but I did not understand why they were so long about launching it, unless they were waiting to cut the other one loose and launch them both at the same time. Two young men of the crew, nice looking, dressed in white, one tall and the other smaller, were coolly debating as to whether the compartments would hold the ship afloat. They were standing with their backs to the rail looking on at the rest of the crew, and I recall asking one of them why he did not assist.

At this time there were other passengers around, but Clinch Smith was the only one associated with me here to the last. It was about this time, fifteen minutes after the launching of the last lifeboat on the port side, that I heard a noise that spread consternation among us all. This was no less than the water striking the bridge and gurgling up the hatchway forward. It seemed momentarily as if it would reach the Boat Deck. It appeared as if it would take the crew a long time to turn the Engelhardt boat right side up and lift it over the rail, and there were so many ready to board her that she would have been swamped. Probably taking these points into consideration, Clinch Smith made the proposition that we should leave and go toward the stern, still on the starboard side, so he started and I followed immediately after him. We had taken but a few steps in the direction indicated when there arose before us from the decks below, a mass of humanity several lines deep, covering the Boat Deck, facing us, and completely blocking our passage toward the stern.

There were women in the crowd, as well as men, and they seemed to be steerage passengers who had just come up from the decks below. Instantly, when they saw us and the water on the deck chasing us from behind, they turned in the opposite direction towards the stern. This brought them at that point plumb against the iron fence and railing which divide the first and second cabin passengers. Even among these people there was no hysterical cry, or evidence of panic, but oh, the agony of it! Clinch Smith and I instantly saw that we could make no progress ahead, and with the water following us behind over the deck, we were in a desperate place. I can never forget the exact point on the ship where he and I were located, viz., at the opening of the angle made by the walls of the officers' house and only a short distance abaft the *Titanic*'s forward 'expansion joint'. Clinch Smith was immediately on my left, nearer the apex of the angle, and our backs were turned toward the ship's rail and the sea. Looking up toward the roof of the officers' house I saw a man to the right of me and above lying on his stomach on the roof, with his legs dangling over. Clinch Smith jumped to reach this roof, and I promptly followed. The efforts of both of us failed. I was loaded down with heavy long-skirted overcoat and Norfolk coat beneath, with clumsy life-preserver over all, which made my jump fall short. As I came down, the water struck my right side. I crouched down into it preparatory to jumping with it, and rose as if on the crest of a wave on the seashore. This expedient brought the attainment of the object I had in view. I was able to reach the roof and the iron railing that is along the edge of it, and pulled myself over on top of the officers' house on my stomach near the base of the second funnel. The feat which I instinctively accomplished was the simple one, familiar to all bathers in the surf at the seashore. I had no time to advise Clinch Smith to adopt it. To my utter dismay, a hasty glance to my left and right showed that he had not followed my example, and that the wave, if I may call it such, which had mounted me to the roof, had completely covered him, as well as all people on both sides of me, including the man I had first seen athwart the roof.

With this second wind under water there came to me a new lease of life and strength, until finally I noticed by the increase of light that I was drawing near to the surface. Though it was not daylight, the clear star-lit night made a noticeable difference in the degree of light immediately below the surface of the water. As I was rising, I came in contact with ascending wreckage, but the only thing I struck of material size was a small plank, which I tucked under my right arm. This circumstance brought with it the reflection that it was advisable for me to secure what best I could to keep me afloat on the surface until succor arrived. When my head at last rose above the water, I detected a piece of wreckage like a wooden crate, and I eagerly seized it as a nucleus of the projected raft to be constructed from what flotsam and jetsam I might collect. Looking about me, I could see no *Titanic* in sight. She had entirely disappeared beneath the calm surface of the ocean and without a sign of any wave. That the sea had swallowed her up with all her precious belongings was indicated by the slight sound of a gulp behind me as the water closed over her. The length of time that I was under water can be estimated by the fact that I sank with her, and when I came up there was no ship in sight. The accounts of others as to the length of time it took the *Titanic* to sink afford the best measure of the interval I was below the surface.

What impressed me at the time that my eyes beheld the horrible scene was a thin light-gray smoky vapor that hung like a pall a few feet above the broad expanse of sea that was covered with a mass of tangled wreckage. That it was a tangible vapor, and not a product of imagination, I feel well assured. It may have been caused by smoke or steam rising to the surface around the area where the ship had sunk. At any rate it produced a supernatural effect, and the pictures I had seen by Dante and the description I had read in my Virgil of the infernal regions, of Charon, and the River Lethe, were then uppermost in my thoughts. Add to this, within the area described, which was as far as my eyes could reach, there arose to the sky the most horrible sounds ever heard by mortal man except by those of us who survived this terrible tragedy. The agonizing cries of death from over a thousand throats, the wails and groans of the suffering, the shrieks of the terror-stricken and the awful gaspings for breath of those in the last throes of drowning, none of us will ever forget to our dying day. 'Help! Help! Boat ahoy! Boat ahoy!' and 'My God! My God!' were the heart-rending cries and shrieks of men, which floated to us over the surface of the dark waters continuously for the next hour, but as time went on, growing weaker and weaker until they died out entirely.

S.S. *Titanic* under construction at Harland and Wolff's Queen's Island shipyard, Belfast, in the spring of 1911, prior to her launch on 31 May

Ulster Folk and Transport Museum Photographic Archive, Harland and Wolff Collection

After a week by the dockside at Southampton, the tugs strain to pull the great ship away as the last rope is released and she sets off on her maiden voyage. The photograph was taken on 10 April 1912 by H.G. Lloyd, a local resident

Ulster Folk and Transport Museum Photographic Archive, Courtney Collection

The *Café Parisienne*, situated on the starboard side of *Titanic's* B Deck, gives an indication of the luxurious facilities available to first-class passengers

Ulster Folk and Transport Museum Photographic Archive, Harland and Wolff Collection

After a ninety minute stop at Cherbourg the previous evening, the *Titanic* arrived off Queenstown (now Cobh) on the south-west coast of Ireland in the early afternoon of 11 April 1912. This photograph was taken by Father Francis Browne, who had travelled from South-ampton, aboard the tender which had brought 113 Irish emigrants to board the ship. The figure looking down from the bridge is Captain Smith; this is the last picture taken of him

The Father Browne S.J. Collection

Edward J. Smith, captain of the *Titanic* (right), photographed in 1911 on board the *Titanic's* sister ship on the White Star Line, the *Olympic*, alongside Lord Pirrie, chairman of Harland and Wolff. Lord Pirrie supervised the design of both vessels, but was prevented by illness from accompanying Captain Smith on the *Titanic's* maiden voyage

Southampton City Museums

Titanic Marconi wireless operators: Mr Jack Phillips (left) who was lost, and Mr Harold Bride who was saved and gave evidence at the British enquiry into the disaster (see p.27)

The Father Browne S.J. Collection

The *Titanic's* surviving stewards and cooks, photographed in Plymouth Docks following their return from America on 29 April 1912. After rescue by S.S. *Carpathia*, they had been taken to New York before their return voyage across the Atlantic aboard the Red Star liner, *Lapland*. They were detained in Plymouth, along with other surviving crew members, until they had supplied statements to be used at the enquiry; some were also required to give evidence in person at the Court in London

Southampton City Museums

The scene at Southampton railway station on the night of 29 April 1912, following the arrival of a special train from Plymouth carrying eighty-five *Titanic* seamen and firemen. Among those pictured returning to their home town is J. Pascoe, seaman (left, with kitbag), reunited with his mother and three brothers

Southampton City Museums

Report on the Loss of the "Titanic" (s.s.)

THE MERCHANT SHIPPING ACTS, 1894 to 1906.

IN THE MATTER OF the Formal Investigation held at the Scottish Hall, Buckingham Gate, Westminster, on the 2nd, 3rd, 7th, 8th, 9th, 10th, 14th, 15th, 16th, 17th, 20th, 21st, 22nd, 23rd and 24th May, the 4th, 5th, 6th, 7th, 10th, 11th, 12th, 13th, 14th, 17th, 18th, 19th, 21st, 24th, 25th, 26th, 27th, 28th and 29th June, at the Caxton Hall, Caxton Street, Westminster, on the 1st and 3rd July, and at the Scottish Hall, Buckingham Gate, Westminster, on the 30th July, 1912, before the Right Honourable Lord Mersey, Wreck Commissioner, assisted by Rear Admiral the Honourable S. A. Gough-Calthorpe, C.V.O., R.N. ; Captain A. W. Clarke ; Commander F. C. A. Lyon, R.N.R. ; Professor J. H. Biles, D.Sc., LL.D., and Mr. E. C. Chaston, R.N.R., as Assessors, into the circumstances attending the loss of the steamship "Titanic," of Liverpool, and the loss of 1,490 lives in the North Atlantic Ocean, in lat. 41° 46′ N., long. 50° 14′ W. on the 15th April last.

REPORT OF THE COURT.

The Court, having carefully enquired into the circumstances of the above mentioned shipping casualty, finds, for the reasons appearing in the Annex hereto, that the loss of the said ship was due to collision with an iceberg, brought about by the excessive speed at which the ship was being navigated.

Dated this 30th day of July, 1912.

MERSEY,

Wreck Commissioner.

We concur in the above Report.

ARTHUR GOUGH-CALTHORPE.

A. W. CLARKE.

F. C. A. LYON.

J. H. BILES.

EDWARD C. CHASTON.

Assessors.

Wt. 15512—251. 3,000. 8/12. J. T. & S.

A

TABLE OF CONTENTS.

ANNEX TO THE REPORT.

INTRODUCTION.

On the 23rd April, 1912, the Lord Chancellor appointed a Wreck Commissioner under the Merchant Shipping Acts, and on the 26th April the Home Secretary nominated five assessors. On the 30th April the Board of Trade requested that a Formal Investigation of the circumstances attending the loss of the Steamship "Titanic" should be held, and the Court accordingly commenced to sit on 2nd May. Since that date there have been thirty-seven public sittings, at which ninety-seven witnesses have been examined, while a large number of documents, charts and plans have been produced. The twenty-six questions formulated by the Board of Trade, which are set out in detail below, appear to cover all the circumstances to be enquired into. Briefly summarised, they deal with the history of the ship, her design, construction, size, speed, general equipment, life-saving apparatus, wireless installation, her orders and course, her passengers, her crew, their training, organisation and discipline; they request an account of the casualty, its cause and effect, and of the means taken for saving those on board the ship; and they call for a report on the efficiency of the Rules and Regulations made by the Board of Trade under the Merchant Shipping Acts and on their administration, and, finally, for any recommendations to obviate similar disasters which may appear to the Court to be desirable. The twenty-six questions as subsequently amended are here attached :—

1. When the "Titanic" left Queenstown on or about 11th April last—

    (a) What was the total number of persons employed in any capacity on board her, and what were their respective ratings?

    (b) What was the total number of her passengers, distinguishing sexes and classes, and discriminating between adults and children?

2. Before leaving Queenstown on or about 11th April last did the "Titanic" comply with the requirements of the Merchant Shipping Acts, 1894-1906, and the rules and regulations made thereunder with regard to the safety and otherwise of "passenger steamers" and "emigrant ships"?

3. In the actual design and construction of the "Titanic" what special provisions were made for the safety of the vessel and the lives of those on board in the event of collisions and other casualties?

4. Was the "Titanic" sufficiently and efficiently officered and manned? Were the watches of the officers and crew usual and proper? Was the "Titanic" supplied with proper charts?

5. What was the number of the boats of any kind on board the "Titanic"? Were the arrangements for manning and launching the boats on board the "Titanic" in case of emergency proper and sufficient? Had a boat drill been held on board, and, if so, when? What was the carrying capacity of the respective boats?

6. What installations for receiving and transmitting messages by wireless telegraphy were on board the "Titanic"? How many operators were employed on working such installations? Were the installations in good and effective working order, and were the number of operators sufficient to enable messages to be received and transmitted continuously by day and night?

7. At or prior to the sailing of the "Titanic" what, if any, instructions as to navigation were given to the master or known by him to apply to her voyage? Were such instructions, if any, safe, proper and adequate, having regard to the time of year and dangers likely to be encountered during the voyage?

8. What was in fact the track taken by the "Titanic" in crossing the Atlantic Ocean? Did she keep to the track usually followed by liners on voyages from the United Kingdom to New York in the month of April? Are such tracks safe tracks at that time of the year? Had the master any, and, if so, what discretion as regards the track to be taken?

9. After leaving Queenstown on or about the 11th April last did information reach the "Titanic" by wireless messages or otherwise by signals of the existence of ice in certain latitudes? If so, what were such messages or signals and when were they received, and in what position or positions was the ice reported to be, and was the ice reported in or near the track actually being followed by the "Titanic"? Was her course altered in consequence of receiving such information, and, if so, in what way? What replies to such messages or signals did the "Titanic" send, and at what times?

10. If at the times referred to in the last preceding question or later the "Titanic" was warned of or had reason to suppose she would encounter ice, at what time might she have reasonably expected to encounter it? Was a good and proper look-out for ice kept on board? Were any, and, if so, what directions given to vary the speed—if so, were they carried out?

11. Were binoculars provided for and used by the look-out men? Is the use of them necessary or usual in such circumstances? Had the "Titanic" the means of throwing searchlights around her? If so, did she make use of them to discover ice? Should searchlights have been provided and used?

12. What other precautions were taken by the "Titanic" in anticipation of meeting ice? Were they such as are usually adopted by vessels being navigated in waters where ice may be expected to be encountered?

13. Was ice seen and reported by anybody on board the "Titanic" before the casualty occurred? If so, what measures were taken by the officer on watch to avoid it? Were they proper measures and were they promptly taken?

14. What was the speed of the "Titanic" shortly before and at the moment of the casualty? Was such speed excessive under the circumstances?

15. What was the nature of the casualty which happened to the "Titanic" at or about 11.45 p.m. on the 14th April last? In what latitude and longitude did the casualty occur?

16. What steps were taken immediately on the happening of the casualty? How long after the casualty was its seriousness realised by those in charge of the vessel? What steps were then taken? What endeavours were made to save the lives of those on board, and to prevent the vessel from sinking?

17. Was proper discipline maintained on board after the casualty occurred?

18. What messages for assistance were sent by the 'Titanic" after the casualty and, at what times respectively? What messages were received by her in response, and at what times respectively? By what vessels were the messages that were sent by the "Titanic" received, and from what vessels did she receive answers? What vessels other than the "Titanic" sent or received messages at or shortly after the casualty in connection with such casualty? What were the vessels that sent or received such messages? Were any vessels prevented from going to the assistance of the "Titanic" or her boats owing to messages received from the "Titanic" or owing to any erroneous messages being sent or received? In regard to such erroneous messages, from what vessels were they sent, and by what vessels were they received and at what times respectively?

19. Was the apparatus for lowering the boats on the " Titanic " at the time of the casualty in good working order? Were the boats swung out, filled, lowered, or otherwise put into the water and got away under proper superintendence? Were the boats sent away in seaworthy condition and properly manned, equipped and provisioned? Did the boats, whether those under davits or otherwise, prove to be efficient and serviceable for the purpose of saving life?

20. What was the number of (a) passengers, (b) crew taken away in each boat on leaving the vessel? How was this number made up, having regard to :—

      1. Sex.
      2. Class.
      3. Rating.

How many were children and how many adults? Did each boat carry its full load, and, if not, why not?

21. How many persons on board the " Titanic " at the time of the casualty were ultimately rescued and by what means? How many lost their lives prior to the arrival of the s.s. " Carpathia " in New York? What was the number of passengers distinguishing between men and women and adults and children of the first, second, and third classes respectively who were saved? What was the number of the crew, discriminating their ratings and sex, that were saved? What is the proportion which each of these numbers bears to the corresponding total number on board immediately before the casualty? What reason is there for the disproportion, if any?

22. What happened to the vessel from the happening of the casualty until she foundered?

23. Where and at what time did the " Titanic " founder?

24. What was the cause of the loss of the " Titanic," and of the loss of life which thereby ensued or occurred? What vessels had the opportunity of rendering assistance to the " Titanic," and, if any, how was it that assistance did not reach the " Titanic " before the s.s. " Carpathia " arrived? Was the construction of the vessel and its arrangements such as to make it difficult for any class of passenger or any portion of the crew to take full advantage of any of the existing provisions for safety?

25. When the " Titanic " left Queenstown on or about 11th April last was she properly constructed and adequately equipped as a passenger steamer and emigrant ship for the Atlantic service?

26. The Court is invited to report upon the Rules and Regulations made under the Merchant Shipping Acts, 1894-1906, and the administration of those Acts and of such Rules and Regulations, so far as the consideration thereof is material to this casualty, and to make any recommendations or suggestions that it may think fit, having regard to the circumstances of the casualty with a view to promoting the safety of vessels and persons at sea.

In framing this Report it has seemed best to divide it into sections in the following manner :—

FIRSTLY.—A description of the ship as she left Southampton on the 10th of April and of her equipment, crew and passengers.

SECONDLY.—An account of her journey across the Atlantic, of the messages she received and of the disaster.

THIRDLY.—A description of the damage to the ship and of its gradual and final effect with observations thereon.

FOURTHLY.—An account of the saving and rescue of those who survived.

FIFTHLY.—The circumstances in connection with the s.s. "Californian."

SIXTHLY.—An account of the Board of Trade's administration.

SEVENTHLY.—The finding of the Court on the questions submitted; and

EIGHTHLY.—The recommendations held to be desirable.

I.—DESCRIPTION OF THE SHIP.

The White Star Line.

The "Titanic" was one of a fleet of thirteen ships employed in the transport of passengers, mails, and cargo between Great Britain and the United States, the usual ports of call for the service in which she was engaged being Southampton, Cherbourg, Plymouth, Queenstown and New York. Sanderson, 19589-97

The owners are the Oceanic Steam Navigation Company, Limited, usually known as the White Star Line, a British registered company, with a capital of £750,000, all paid up, the directors being Mr. J. Bruce Ismay (Chairman), the Right Hon. Lord Pirrie, and Mr. H. A. Sanderson. Ismay, 18224-69

The Company are owners of twenty-nine steamers and tenders; they have a large interest in thirteen other steamers, and also own a training sailing ship for officers.

All the shares of the Company, with the exception of eight held by Messrs. E. C. Grenfell, Vivian H. Smith, W. S. M. Burns, James Gray, J. Bruce Ismay, H. A. Sanderson, A. Kerr and the Right Hon. Lord Pirrie, have, since the year 1902, been held by the International Navigation Company, Limited, of Liverpool, a British registered company, with a capital of £700,000, of which all is paid up, the directors being Mr. J. Bruce Ismay (Chairman), and Messrs. H. A. Sanderson, Charles F. Torrey and H. Concanon.

The debentures of the Company, £1,250,000, are held mainly, if not entirely, in the United Kingdom by the general public.

The International Navigation Company, Limited, of Liverpool, in addition to holding the above-mentioned shares of the Oceanic Steam Navigation Company, Limited, is also the owner of :—

1. Practically the whole of the issued share capital of the British and North Atlantic Steam Navigation Company, Limited, and the Mississippi and Dominion Steamship Company, Limited (the Dominion Line).

2. Practically the whole of the issued share capital of the Atlantic Transport Company, Limited (the Atlantic Transport Line).

3. Practically the whole of the issued ordinary share capital and about one-half of the preference share capital of Frederick Leyland and Company, Limited (the Leyland Line).

As against the above-mentioned shares and other property, the International Navigation Company, Limited, have issued share lien certificates for £25,000,000.

Both the shares and share lien certificates of the International Navigation Company, Limited, are now held by the International Mercantile Marine Company of New Jersey, or by trustees for the holders of its debenture bonds.

The Steamship "Titanic."

The "Titanic" was a three-screw vessel of 46,328 tons gross and 21,831 net register tons, built by Messrs. Harland and Wolff for the White Star Line service between Southampton and New York. She was registered as a British steamship at the port of Liverpool, her official number being 131,428. Her registered dimensions were :— Wilding, 19789 et seq.

Length	852·5 ft.
Breadth	92·5 „
Depth from top of keel to top of beam at lowest point of sheer of C. Deck, the highest deck which extends continuously from bow to stern	64 ft. 9 in.
Depth of hold	59·58 ft.
Height from B to C deck	9·0 „
„ „ A to B „	9·0 „
„ „ Boat to A deck	9·5 „
„ „ Boat deck to waterline amidships at time of accident about	60·5 „
Displacement at 34 ft. 7 in. is	52,310 tons.

The propelling machinery consisted of two sets of four-cylinder reciprocating engines, each driving a wing propeller, and a turbine driving the centre propeller. The registered horse-power of the propelling machinery was 50,000. The power which would probably have been developed was at least 55,000.

Structural arrangements—The structural arrangements of the "Titanic" consisted primarily of :—

(1) An outer shell of steel plating, giving form to the ship up to the top decks.

(2) Steel Decks.—These were enumerated as follows :—

	Height to next deck above.	Distance from 34 ft. 7 in. water line amidships.	
		Above.	Below.
	ft. in.	ft. in.	ft. in.
Boat deck, length about 500 ft. ...	—	58 0	—
A „ „ „ 500 „ ...	9 6	48 6	—
B „ „ „ 550 „ with 125 ft. forecastle and 105 ft. poop	9 0	39 6	—
C deck, whole length of ship ...	9 0	30 6	—
D „ „ „ „ ...	10 6	20 0 (tapered down at ends)	—
E „ „ „ „ ...	9 0	11 0	—
F „ „ „ „ ...	8 6	2 6	—
G deck, 190 ft. forward of boilers, 210 ft. aft of machinery	8 0	—	5 6
Orlop deck, 190 ft. forward of boilers, 210 ft. aft of machinery	8 0	—	13 6

C, D, E and F were continuous from end to end of the ship. The decks above these were continuous for the greater part of the ship, extending from amidships both forward and aft. The Boat deck and A deck each had two expansion joints, which broke the strength continuity. The decks below were continuous outside the boiler and engine-rooms and extended to the ends of the ship. Except in small patches none of these decks was watertight in the steel parts, except the weather deck and the orlop deck aft.

(3) Transverse Vertical Bulkheads.—There were 15 transverse watertight bulkheads, by which the ship was divided in the direction of her length into 16 separate compartments. These bulkheads are referred to as "A" to "P," commencing forward.

The watertightness of the bulkheads extended up to one or other of the decks D or E; the bulkhead A extended to C, but was only watertight to D deck. The position of the D, E and F decks, which were the only ones to which the watertight bulkheads extended was in relation to the waterline (34 ft. 7 in. draught) approximately as follows :—

	Height above waterline (34 ft. 7 in.).		
	lowest part amidships.	at bow.	at stern.
	ft. in.	ft. in.	ft. in.
D	20 0 ...	33 0 ...	25 0
E	11 0 ...	24 0 ...	16 0
F	2 6 ...	15 6 ...	7 6

These were the three of the four decks which, as already stated, were continuous all fore and aft. The other decks, G and Orlop, which extended only along a part of the ship, were spaced about 8 ft. apart. The G deck forward was about 7 ft. 6 in. above the waterline at the bow and about level with the waterline at bulkhead D, which was at the fore end of boilers. The G deck aft and the Orlop deck at both ends of the vessel were below the waterline. The Orlop deck abaft of the turbine engine-room and forward of the collision bulkhead was watertight. Elsewhere, except in very small patches, the decks were not watertight. All the decks had large openings or hatchways in them in each compartment, so that water could rise freely through them.

There was also a watertight inner bottom, or tank top, about 5 ft. above the top of the keel, which extended for the full breadth of the vessel from bulkhead A to 20 ft. before bulkhead P—i.e., for the whole length of the vessel except a small distance at each end. The transverse watertight divisions of this double bottom practically coincided with the watertight transverse bulkheads; there was an additional watertight division under the middle of the reciprocating engine-room compartment (between bulkheads K and L). There were three longitudinal watertight divisions in the double bottom, one at the centre of the ship, extending for about 670 ft., and one on each side, extending for 447 ft.

All the transverse bulkheads were carried up watertight to at least the height of the E deck. Bulkheads A and B, and all bulkheads from K (90 ft. abaft amidships) to P, both inclusive, further extended watertight up to the underside of D deck. A bulkhead further extended to C deck, but it was watertight only to D deck.

Bulkheads A and B forward, and P aft, had no openings in them. All the other bulkheads had openings in them, which were fitted with watertight doors. Bulkheads D to O, both inclusive, had each a vertical sliding watertight door at the level of the floor of the engine and boiler rooms for the use of the engineers and firemen. On the Orlop deck there was one door, on bulkhead N, for access to the refrigerator rooms. On G deck there were no watertight doors in the bulkheads. On both the F and E decks nearly all the bulkheads had watertight doors, mainly for giving communication between the different blocks of passenger accommodation. All the doors, except those in the engine rooms and boiler rooms, were horizontal sliding doors workable by hand both at the door and at the deck above.

There were twelve vertical sliding watertight doors which completed the watertightness of bulkheads D to O inclusive, in the boiler and engine rooms. These were capable of being simultaneously closed from the bridge. The operation of closing was intended to be preceded by the ringing from the bridge of a warning bell.

These doors were closed by the bringing into operation of an electric current and could not be opened until this current was cut off from the bridge. When this was done the doors could only be opened by a mechanical operation manually worked separately at each door. They could, however, be individually lowered again by operating a lever at the door. In addition they would be automatically closed, if open, should water enter the compartment. This operation was done in each case by means of a float actuated by the water which was in either of the compartments which happened to be in the process of being flooded.

There were no sluice valves or means of letting water from one compartment to another.

Detailed description.

The following is a more detailed description of the vessel, her passenger and crew accommodation, and her machinery.

Watertight compartments.

The following table shows the decks to which the bulkheads extended, and the numbers of doors in them:—

Bulkhead letter.	Extends up to under side of Deck.	Engine and boiler spaces (all controlled from bridge).	Orlop to G deck.	F to E deck.	E to D deck.
A	C				
B	D				
C	E			1	
D	E	*1		1	
E	E	†1			
F	E	†1		2	
G	E	†1			
H	E	†1		2	
J	E	†1		2	
K	D	1			2
L	D	1			2
M	D	1		1	2
N	D	1	1	1	2
O	D	1			1
P	D				

* There was another watertight door at the after end of the watertight passage through the bunker immediately aft of "D" bulkhead. This door and the one on the "D" bulkhead formed a double protection to the forward boiler room.

† The watertight doors for these bulkheads were not on them, but were at the end of a watertight passage (about 9 feet long), leading from the bulkhead through the bunker into the compartment.

The following table shows the actual contents of each separate watertight compartment. The compartments are shown in the left column, the contents of each compartment being read off horizontally. The contents of each watertight compartment is separately given in the deck space in which it is :—

W.T. compt.	Length of each W.T. compt. in fore and aft direction.	Hold.	Orlop to G deck.	G to F deck.	F to E deck.	E to D deck.
Bow to A	46 ft.	Fore peak tank (not used excepting for trimming ship)	Fore peak store room .	Fore peak store room.	Fore peak store room.	Fore peak store room.
A–B	45 ft.	Cargo ...	Cargo ...	Living spaces for firemen, &c.	Living spaces for firemen.	Living spaces for firemen.
B–C	51 ft.	Do. ...	Do. ...	3rd class passenger accommodation.	3rd class passenger accommodation.	3rd class passenger and seamen's spaces.
C–D	51 ft.	Alternatively coal and cargo	Luggage and mails.	Baggage, squash rackets and 3rd class passengers.	3rd class passenger accommodation.	3rd class passenger accommodation.
D–E	54 ft.	No. 6 boiler room	No. 6 boiler room.	Coal and boiler casing.	3rd class passenger accommodation.	1st class passenger accommodation.
E–F	57 ft.	No. 5 do. ...	No. 5 do. ...	Coal bunker and boiler casing and swimming bath.	Linen rooms and swimming bath.	1st class passenger accommodation.
F–G	57 ft.	No. 4 do. ...	No. 4 do. ...	Coal bunker and boiler casing.	Stewards, Turkish baths, &c.	1st class and stewards.
G–H	57 ft.	No. 3 do. ...	No. 3 do. ...	Coal bunker and boiler casing.	3rd class saloon.	1st and 2nd class and stewards.
H–J	60 ft.	No. 2 do. ...	No. 2 do. ...	Coal bunker and boiler casing.	3rd class saloon.	1st class
J–K	36 ft.	No. 1 do. ...	No. 1 do. ...	Coal bunker and boiler casing.	3rd class galley, stewards, &c.	1st class and stewards.
K–L	69 ft.	Recipg. engine room.	Recipg. engine room.	Reciprocating engine room casing, workshop and engineers' stores	Engineers' and reciprocating engine casing.	1st class and engineers' mess, &c.
L–M	57 ft.	Turbine engine room.	Turbine engine room.	Turbine engine room casing and small stewards' strs.	2nd class and turbine eng. room casing.	2nd class and stewards, &c.
M–N	63 ft.	Electric engine room.	Provisions and electric engine casing.	Provisions ...	2nd class ...	2nd and 3rd class.
N–O	54 ft.	Tunnel ...	Refrigerated cargo.	3rd class ...	2nd class ...	2nd and 3rd class.
O–P	57 ft.	Do.	Cargo.	3rd class ...	3rd class ...	3rd class
P to Stern.	36 ft.	After pk. tank for trimming ship	After pk. tank for trimming ship.	Stores ...	Stores ...	Stores

The vessel was constructed under survey of the British Board of Trade for a passenger certificate, and also to comply with the American Immigration Laws.

Steam was supplied from six entirely independent groups of boilers in six separate watertight compartments. The after boiler room No. 1 contained five single-ended boilers. Four other boiler rooms, Nos. 2, 3, 4 and 5, each contained five double-ended boilers. The forward boiler room, No. 6, contained four double-ended boilers. The reciprocating engines and most of the auxiliary machinery were in a seventh separate watertight compartment aft of the boilers; the low-pressure turbine, the main condensers and the thrust blocks of the reciprocating engine were in an eighth separate watertight compartment. The main electrical machinery was in a ninth separate watertight compartment immediately abaft the turbine engine room. Two emergency steam-driven dynamos were placed on the D deck, 21 ft. above the level of the load water-line. These dynamos were arranged to take their supply of steam from any of the three of the boiler rooms Nos. 2, 3 and 5, and were intended to be available in the event of the main dynamo room being flooded.

The ship was equipped with the following :—

(1) Wireless telegraphy.

(2) Submarine signalling.

(3) Electric lights and power systems.

(4) Telephones for communication between the different working positions in the vessel. In addition to the telephones, the means of communication included engine and docking telegraphs, and duplicate or emergency engine-room telegraph, to be used in the event of any accident to the ordinary telegraph.

(5) Three electric elevators for taking passengers in the first class up to A deck, immediately below the Boat deck, and one in the second class for taking passengers up to the Boat deck.

(6) Four electrically-driven boat winches on the Boat deck for hauling up the boats.

(7) Life-saving appliances to the requirements of the Board of Trade, including boats and life belts.

(8) Steam whistles on the two foremost funnels, worked on the Willett-Bruce system of automatic control.

(9) Navigation appliances, including Kelvin's patent sounding machines for finding the depth of water under the ship without stopping; Walker's taffrail log for determining the speed of the ship; and flash signal lamps fitted above the shelters at each end of the navigating bridge for Morse signalling with other ships.

Decks and Accommodation.

The Boat Deck was an uncovered deck, on which the boats were placed. At its lowest point it was about 92 ft. 6 in. above the keel. The overall length of this deck was about 500 ft. The forward end of it was fitted to serve as the navigating bridge of the vessel and was 190 ft. from the bow. On the after end of the bridge was a wheel house, containing the steering wheel and a steering compass. The chart room was immediately abaft this. On the starboard side of the wheel house and funnel casing were the navigating room, the captain's quarters, and some officers' quarters. On the port side were the remainder of the officers' quarters. At the middle line abaft the forward funnel casing were the wireless telegraphy rooms and the operators' quarters. The top of the officers' house formed a short deck. The connections from the Marconi aerials were made on this deck, and two of the collapsible boats were placed on it. Aft of the officers' house were the first-class passengers' entrance and stairways, and other adjuncts to the passengers' accommodation below. These stairways had a minimum effective width of 8 ft. They had assembling landings at the level of each deck, and three elevators communicating from E to A decks, but not to the Boat deck, immediately on the fore side of the stairway.

All the boats except two Engelhardt life rafts were carried on this deck. There were seven lifeboats on each side, 30 ft. long, 9 ft. wide. There was an emergency cutter, 25 ft. long, on each side at the fore end of the deck. Abreast of each cutter was an Engelhardt life raft. One similar raft was carried on the top of the officers' house on each side. In all there were 14 lifeboats, 2 cutters, and 4 Engelhardt life rafts.

The forward group of four boats and one Engelhardt raft were placed on each side of the deck alongside the officers' quarters and the first-class entrance. Further aft at the middle line on this deck was the special platform for the standard compass. At the after end of this deck was an entrance house for second-class passengers, with a stairway and elevator leading directly down to F deck. There were two vertical iron ladders at the after end of this deck, leading to A deck, for the use of the crew. Alongside and immediately forward of the second-class entrance was the after group of lifeboats, four on each side of the ship.

In addition to the main stairways mentioned, there was a ladder on each side amidships, giving access from the A deck below. At the forward end of the Boat deck there was on each side a ladder leading up from A deck, with a landing there, from which, by a ladder, access to B deck could be obtained direct. Between the reciprocating engine casing and the third funnel casing there was a stewards' stairway, which communicated with all the decks below as far as E deck. Outside the deck houses was promenading space for first class passengers.

A Deck.—The next deck below the boat deck was A deck. It extended over a length of about 500 feet. On this deck was a long house, extending nearly the whole length of the deck. It was of irregular shape, varying in width from 24 ft. to 72 ft. At the forward end it contained 34 state-rooms, and abaft these a number of public rooms, etc., for first-class passengers, including two first-class entrances and stairway, reading-room, lounge and the smoke-room. Outside the deck house was a promenade for first-class passengers. The forward end of it on both sides of the ship, below the forward group of boats and for a short distance further aft, was protected against the weather by a steel screen, 192 ft. long, with large windows in it. In addition to the stairway described on the Boat deck, there was near the after-end of the A deck, and immediately forward of the first-class smoke-room, another first-class entrance, giving access as far down as C deck. The second-class stairway at the after-end of this deck (already described under the Boat deck) had no exit on to the A deck. The stewards' staircase opened on to this deck.

B Deck—The next lowest deck was B deck, which constituted the top deck of the strong structure of the vessel, the decks above and the side plating between them being light plating. This deck extended continuously for 550 ft. There were breaks or wells both forward and aft of it, each about 50 ft. long. It was terminated by a poop and forecastle. On this deck were placed the principal state-rooms of the vessel, 97 in number, having berths for 198 passengers, and aft of these was the first-class stairway and reception-room, as well as the restaurant for first-class passengers and its pantry and galley. Immediately aft of this restaurant were the second-class stairway and smoke-room. At the forward end of the deck outside the house was an assembling area, giving access by the ladders, previously mentioned, leading directly to the Boat deck. From this same space a ladderway led to the forward third-class promenade on C deck. At the after-end of it were two ladders giving access to the after third-class promenade on C deck. At the after-end of this deck, at the middle line, was placed another second-class stairway, which gave access to C, D, E, F and G decks.

At the forward end of the vessel, on the level of the B deck, was situated the forecastle deck, which was 125 ft. long. On it were placed the gear for working the anchors and cables and for warping (or moving) the ship in dock. At the after-end, on the same level, was the poop deck, about 105 ft. long, which carried the after-warping appliances and was a third-class promenading space. Arranged above the poop was a light docking bridge, with telephone, telegraphs, etc., communicating to the main navigating bridge forward.

C Deck.—The next lowest deck was C deck. This was the highest deck which extended continuously from bow to stern. At the forward end of it, under the forecastle, was placed the machinery required for working the anchors and cables and for the warping of the ship referred to on B deck above: there were also the crew's galley and the seamen's and firemen's mess-room accommodation, where their meals were taken. At the after-end of the forecastle, at each side of the ship, were the entrances to the third-class spaces below. On the port side, at the extreme after-end and opening on to the deck, was the lamp-room. The break in B deck between the forecastle and the first-class passenger quarters formed a well about 50 ft. in length, which enabled the space under it on C deck to be used as a third-class promenade. This space contained two hatchways, the No. 2 hatch and the bunker hatch. The latter of these hatchways gave access to the space allotted to the first and second-class baggage hold, the mails, specie and parcel room, and to the lower hold, which was used for cargo or coals. Abaft of this well there was a house 450 ft. long and extending for the full breadth of the ship. It contained

148 state-rooms for first class, besides service rooms of various kinds. On this deck, at the forward first-class entrance, were the purser's office and the enquiry office, where passengers' telegrams were received for sending by the Marconi apparatus. Exit doors through the ship's side were fitted abreast of this entrance. Abaft the after-end of this long house was a promenade at the ship's side for second-class passengers, sheltered by bulwarks and bulkheads. In the middle of the promenade stood the second-class library. The two second-class stairways were at the ends of the library, so that from the promenade access was obtained at each end to a second-class main stairway. There was also access by a door from this space into each of the alleyways in the first-class accommodation on each side of the ship, and by two doors at the after-end into the after-well. This after-well was about 50 ft. in length and contained two hatchways called No. 5 and No. 6 hatches. Abaft this well, under the poop, was the main third-class entrance for the after-end of the vessel, leading directly down to G deck, with landings and access at each deck. The effective width of this stairway was 16 ft. to E deck. From E to F it was 8 ft. wide. Aft of this entrance on B deck were the third-class smoke-room and the general room. Between these rooms and the stern was the steam steering gear and the machinery for working the after-capstan gear, which was used for warping the after-end of the vessel. The steam steering gear had three cylinders. The engines were in duplicate, to provide for the possibility of breakdown of one set.

D Deck.—The general height from D deck to C deck was 10 ft. 6 in., this being reduced to 9 ft. at the forward end, and 9 ft. 6 in. at the after end, the taper being obtained gradually by increasing the sheer of the D deck. The forward end of this deck provided accommodation for 108 firemen, who were in two separate watches. There was the necessary lavatory accommodation, abaft the firemen's quarters at the sides of the ship. On each side of the middle line immediately abaft the firemen's quarters there was a vertical spiral staircase leading to the forward end of a tunnel, immediately above the tank top, which extended from the foot of the staircase to the forward stokehole, so that the firemen could pass direct to their work without going through any passenger accommodation or over any passenger decks. On D deck abaft of this staircase was the third class promenade space which was covered in by C deck. From this promenade space there were four separate ladderways with two ladders, 4 ft. wide to each. One ladderway on each side forward led to C deck, and one, the starboard, led to E deck and continued to F deck as a double ladder and to G deck as a single ladder. The two ladderways at the after end led to E deck on both sides and to F deck on the port side. Abaft this promenade space came a block of 50 first-class staterooms. This surrounded the forward funnel. The main first-class reception room and dining saloon were aft of these rooms and surrounded the No. 2 funnel. The reception room and staircase occupied 83 ft. of the length of the ship. The dining saloon occupied 112 ft., and was between the second and third funnels. Abaft this came the first-class pantry, which occupied 56 ft. of the length of the ship. The reciprocating engine hatch came up through this pantry.

Aft of the first-class pantry, the galley, which provides for both first and second-class passengers, occupied 45 ft. of the length of the ship. Aft of this were the turbine engine hatch and the emergency dynamos. Abaft of and on the port side of this hatch were the second-class pantry and other spaces used for the saloon service of the passengers. On the starboard side abreast of these there was a series of rooms used for hospitals and their attendants. These spaces occupied about 54 ft. of the length. Aft of these was the second-class saloon occupying 70 ft. of the length. In the next 88 ft. of length there were 38 second-class rooms and the necessary baths and lavatories. From here to the stern was accommodation for third-class passengers and the main third-class lavatories for the passengers in the after end of the ship. The watertight bulkheads come up to this deck throughout the length from the stern as far forward as the bulkhead dividing the after boiler room from the reciprocating engine room. The watertight bulkhead of the two compartments abaft the stem was carried up to this deck.

E Deck.—The watertight bulkheads, other than those mentioned as extending to D deck, all stopped at this deck. At the forward end was provided accommodation for three watches of trimmers, in three separate compartments, each holding 24 trimmers. Abaft this, on the port side, was accommodation for 44 seamen. Aft of this, and also on the starboard side of it, were the lavatories for crew and third-class passengers; further aft again came the forward third-class lavatories. Immediately aft of this was a passageway right across the ship communicating directly with the ladderways leading to the decks above and below and gangway doors in the ship's side. This passage was 9 ft. wide at the sides and 15 ft. at the centre of the ship.

From the after end of this cross passage main alleyways on each side of the ship ran right through to the after end of the vessel. That on the port side was about $8\frac{1}{2}$ ft. wide. It was the general communication passage for the crew and third-class passengers and was known as the "working passage." In this passage at the centre line in the middle of the length of the ship direct access was obtained to the third-class dining rooms on the deck below by means of a ladderway 20 ft. wide. Between the working passage and the ship's side was the accommodation for the petty officers, most of the stewards, and the engineers' mess room. This accommodation extended for 475 ft. From this passage access was obtained to both engine rooms and the engineers' accommodation, some third-class lavatories and also some third-class accommodation at the after end. There was another cross passage at the end of this accommodation about 9 ft. wide, terminating in gangway doors on each side of the ship. The port side of it was for third-class passengers and the starboard for second class. A door divided the parts, but it could be opened for any useful purpose, or for an emergency. The second-class stairway leading to the Boat deck was in the cross passage way.

The passage on the starboard side ran through the first and then the second-class accommodation, and the forward main first-class stairway and elevators extended to this deck, whilst both the second-class main stairways were also in communication with this starboard passage. There were four first-class, eight first or second alternatively, and 19 second-class rooms leading off this starboard passage.

The remainder of the deck was appropriated to third-class accommodation. This contained the bulk of the third-class accommodation. At the forward end of it was the accommodation for 53 firemen constituting the third watch. Aft of this in three watertight compartments there was third-class accommodation extending to 147 ft. In the next watertight compartment were the swimming bath and linen rooms. In the next watertight compartments were stewards' accommodation on the port side, and the Turkish baths on the starboard side. The next two watertight compartments each contained a third-class dining room.

The third-class stewards' accommodation together with the third-class galley and pantries, filled the watertight compartment. The engineers' accommodation was in the next compartment directly alongside the casing of the reciprocating engine room. The next three compartments were allotted to 64 second-class state rooms. These communicated direct with the second-class main stairways. The after compartments contained third-class accommodation. All spaces on this deck had direct ladderway communication with the deck above, so that if it became necessary to close the watertight doors in the bulkheads an escape was available in all cases. On this deck in way of the boiler rooms were placed the electrically-driven fans which provided ventilation to the stokeholds.

G Deck.—The forward end of this deck had accommodation for 15 leading firemen and 30 greasers. The next watertight compartment contained third-class accommodation in 26 rooms for 106 people. The next watertight compartment contained the first-class baggage room, the post office accommodation, a racquet court, and seven third-class rooms for 34 passengers. From this point to the after end of the boiler room the space was used for the 'tween deck bunkers. Alongside the reciprocating engine room were the engineers' stores and workshop. Abreast of the turbine engine room were some of the ship's stores. In the next watertight compartment abaft the turbine room were the main body of the stores. The next two compartments were appropriated to 186 third-class passengers in 60 rooms; this deck was the lowest on which any passengers or crew were carried.

Below G Deck were two partial decks, the Orlop and Lower Orlop decks, the latter extending only through the fore peak and No. 1 hold; on the former deck, abaft the turbine engine-room, were some store-rooms containing stores for ship's use.

Below these decks again came the inner bottom, extending fore and aft through about nine-tenths of the vessel's length, and on this were placed the boilers, main and auxiliary machinery and the electric light machines. In the remaining spaces below G deck were cargo holds or 'tween decks, seven in all, six forward and one aft. The firemen's passage, giving direct access from their accommodation to the forward boiler room by stairs at the forward end, contained the various pipes and valves connected with the pumping arrangements at the forward end of the ship, and also the steam pipes conveying steam to the windlass gear forward and exhaust steam pipes leading from winches and other deck machinery. It was made thoroughly watertight throughout its length, and at its after-end was closed by a watertight vertical sliding door of the same character as other doors on the inner bottom. Special arrangements were made for pumping this space out, if necessary. The pipes were placed in this tunnel to protect them from possible damage by coal or cargo, and also to facilitate access to them.

On the decks was provided generally, in the manner above described, accommodation for a maximum number of 1,034 first-class passengers, and at the same time 510 second-class passengers and 1,022 third-class passengers. Some of the accommodation was of an alternative character, and could be used for either of two classes of passengers. In the statement of figures the higher alternative class has been reckoned. This makes a total accommodation for 2,566 passengers.

Accommodation was provided for the crew as follows : about 75 of the deck department, including officers and doctors, 326 of the engine-room department, including engineers, and 544 of the victualling department, including pursers and leading stewards.

Access of passengers to the Boat deck.—The following routes led directly from the various parts of the first-class passenger accommodation to the Boat deck : From the forward ends of A, B, C, D, and E decks by the staircase in the forward first-class entrance direct to the Boat deck. The elevators led from the same decks as far as A deck, where further access was obtained by going up the top flight of the main staircase.

The same route was available for first-class passengers forward of midships on B, C, and E decks.

First-class passengers abaft amidships on B and C decks could use the staircase in the after main entrance to A deck, and then could pass out on to the deck, and by the midships stairs besides the house ascend to the Boat deck. They could also use the stewards' staircase between the reciprocating engine casing and Nos. 1 and 2 boiler casing, which led direct to the Boat deck. This last route was also available for passengers on E deck in the same divisions who could use the forward first-class main stairway and elevators.

Second-class passengers on D deck could use their own after-stairway to B deck, and could then pass up their forward stairway to the Boat deck, or else could cross their saloon and use the same stairway throughout.

Of the second-class passengers on E deck, those abreast of the reciprocating engine casing, unless the watertight door immediately abaft them was closed, went aft and joined the other second-class passengers. If, however, the watertight door at the end of their compartment was closed, they passed through an emergency door into the engine-room, and directly up to the Boat deck, by the ladders and gratings in the engine-room casing.

The second-class passengers on E deck in the compartment abreast the turbine casing on the starboard side, and also those on F deck on both sides below could pass through M watertight bulkhead to the forward second-class main stairway. If this door were closed, they could pass by the stairway up to the serving space at the forward end of the second-class saloon, and go into the saloon and thence up the forward second-class stairway.

Passengers between M and N bulkheads on both E and F decks could pass directly up to the forward second-class stairway to the Boat deck.

Passengers between N and O bulkheads on D, E, F and G decks could pass by the after second-class stairway to B deck, and then cross to the forward second-class stairway and go up to the Boat deck.

Third-class passengers at the fore end of the vessel could pass by the staircases to C deck in the forward well and by ladders on the port and starboard sides at the forward end of the deck-houses, thence direct to the Boat deck outside the officers' accommodation. They might also pass along the working passage on E deck and through the emergency door to the forward first-class main stairway, or through the door on the same deck at the forward end of the first-class alleyway and up the first-class stairway direct to the Boat deck.

The third-class passengers at the after-end of the ship passed up their stairway to E deck, and into the working passage, and through the emergency doors to the two second-class stairways, and so to the Boat deck, like second-class passengers. Or, alternatively, they could continue up their own stairs and entrance to C deck, thence by the two ladders at the after-end of the bridge on to the B deck, and thence by the forward second-class stairway direct to the Boat deck.

Crew.—From each boiler-room an escape or emergency ladder was provided direct to the Boat deck by the fidleys, in the boiler casings, and also into the working passage on E deck, and thence by the stair immediately forward of the reciprocating engine casing, direct to the Boat deck.

From both the engine-rooms ladders and gratings gave direct access to the Boat deck.

From the electric engine room, the after tunnels, and the forward pipe tunnels, escapes were provided direct to the working passage on E deck, and thence by one of the several routes already detailed from that space.

From the crew's quarters they could go forward by their own staircases into the forward well, and thence, like the third-class passengers, to the Boat deck.

The stewards' accommodation being all connected to the working passage or the forward main first-class stairway, they could use one of the routes from thence.

The engineers' accommodation also communicated with the working passage, but, as it was possible for them to be shut between two watertight bulkheads, they had also a direct route by the gratings in the engine room casing to the Boat deck.

On all the principal accommodation decks the alleyways and stairways provided a ready means of access to the Boat deck, and there were clear deck spaces in way of all first, second and third-class main entrances and stairways on Boat deck and all decks below.

Structure.

The vessel was built throughout of steel and had a cellular double bottom of the usual type, with a floor at every frame, its depth at the centre line being 63 in., except in way of the reciprocating machinery, where it was 78 in. For about half of the length of the vessel this double bottom extended up the ship's side to a height of 7 ft. above the keel. Forward and aft of the machinery space the protection of the inner bottom extended to a less height above the keel. It was so divided that there were four separate watertight compartments in the breadth of the vessel. Before and abaft the machinery space there was a watertight division at the centre line only, except in the foremost and aftermost tanks. Above the double bottom the vessel was constructed on the usual transverse frame system, reinforced by web frames, which extended to the highest decks.

At the forward end the framing and plating was strengthened with a view to preventing panting, and damage when meeting thin harbour ice.

Beams were fitted on every frame at all decks, from the Boat deck downwards. An external bilge keel, about 300 ft. long and 25 in. deep, was fitted along the bilge amidships.

The heavy ship's plating was carried right up to the Boat deck, and between the C and B deck was doubled. The stringer or edge plate of the B deck was also doubled. This double plating was hydraulic riveted.

All decks were steel plated throughout.

The transverse strength of the ship was in part dependent on the 15 transverse watertight bulkheads, which were specially stiffened and strengthened to enable them to stand the necessary pressure in the event of accident, and they were connected by double angles to decks, inner bottom, and shell plating.

The two decks above the B deck were of comparatively light scantling, but strong enough to ensure their proving satisfactory in these positions in rough weather.

Watertight Sub-division.—In the preparation of the design of this vessel it was arranged that the bulkheads and divisions should be so placed that the ship would remain afloat in the event of any two adjoining compartments being flooded, and that they should be so built and strengthened that the ship would remain afloat under this condition. The minimum freeboard that the vessel would have, in the event of any two compartments being flooded, was between 2 ft. 6 in. and 3 ft. from the deck adjoining the top of the watertight bulkheads. With this object in view 15 watertight bulkheads were arranged in the vessel. The lower part of C bulkhead was doubled, and was in the form of a cofferdam. So far as possible the bulkheads were carried up in one plane to their upper sides, but in cases where they had for any reason to be stepped forward or aft, the deck, in way of the step, was made into a watertight flat, thus completing the watertightness of the compartment. In addition to this, G deck in the after peak was made a watertight flat. The Orlop deck between bulkheads which formed the top of the tunnel was also watertight. The Orlop deck in the forepeak tank was also a watertight flat. The electric machinery compartment was further protected by a structure some distance in from the ship's side, forming six separate watertight compartments, which were used for the storage of fresh water.

Where openings were required for the working of the ship in these watertight bulkheads they were closed by watertight sliding doors which could be worked from a position above the top of the watertight bulkhead, and those doors immediately the inner bottom were of a special automatic closing pattern, as described below. By this sub-division there were in all 73 compartments, 29 of these being above the inner bottom.

Watertight doors.—The doors (12 in number) immediately above the inner bottom were in the engine and boiler room spaces. They were of Messrs. Harland and Wolff's latest type, working vertically. The doorplate was of cast iron of heavy section, strongly ribbed. It closed by gravity, and was held in the open position by a clutch which could be released by means of a powerful electro-magnet controlled from the captain's bridge. In the event of accident, or at any time when it might be considered desirable, the captain or officer on duty could, by simply moving an electric switch, immediately close all these doors. The time required for the doors to close was between 25 and 30 seconds. Each door could also be closed from below by operating a hand lever fitted alongside the door. As a further precaution floats were provided beneath the floor level, which, in the event of water accidentally entering any of the compartments, automatically lifted and thus released the clutches, thereby permitting the doors in that particular compartment to close if they had not already been dropped by any other means. These doors were fitted with cataracts which controlled the speed of closing. Due notice of closing from the bridge was given by a warning bell.

A ladder or escape was provided in each boiler room, engine room and similar watertight compartment, in order that the closing of the doors at any time should not imprison the men working therein.

The watertight doors on E deck were of horizontal pattern, with wrought steel door plates. Those on F deck and the one aft on the Orlop deck were of similar type, but had cast iron door plates of heavy section, strongly ribbed. Each of the 'tween deck doors, and each of the vertical doors on the tank top level could be operated by the ordinary hand gear from the deck above the top of the watertight bulkhead, and from a position on the next deck above, almost directly above the door. To facilitate the quick closing of the doors, plates were affixed in suitable positions on the sides of the alleyways indicating the positions of the deck plates, and a box spanner was provided for each door, hanging in suitable clips alongside the deck plate.

Ship's Side Doors.—Large side doors were provided through the side plating, giving access to passengers' or crew's accommodation as follows :—

On the saloon (D) deck on the starboard side in the forward third-class open space, one baggage door.

In way of the forward first-class entrance, two doors close together on each side.

On the upper (E) deck, one door each side at the forward end of the working passage.

On the port side abreast the engine room, one door leading into the working passage. One door each side on the port and starboard sides aft into the forward second-class entrance.

All the doors on the upper deck were secured by lever handles, and were made watertight by means of rubber strips. Those on the saloon deck were closed by lever handles but had no rubber.

Accommodation Ladder.—One teak accommodation ladder was provided, and could be worked on either side of the ship in the gangway door opposite the second-class entrance on the upper deck (E). It had a folding platform and portable stanchions, hand rope, etc. The ladder extended to within 3 ft. 6 in. of the vessel's light draft, and was stowed overhead in the entrance abreast the forward second-class main staircase. Its lower end was arranged so as to be raised and lowered from a davit immediately above.

Masts and Rigging.—The vessel was rigged with two masts, and fore and aft sails. The two pole masts were constructed of steel, and stiffened with angle irons. The poles at the top of the mast were made of teak.

A look-out cage, constructed of steel, was fitted on the foremast at a height of about 95 ft. above the water line. Access to the cage was obtained by an iron vertical ladder inside of the foremast, with an opening at C deck and one at the look-out cage. An iron ladder was fitted on the foremast from the hounds to the mast-head light.

Life-saving Appliances.

Lifebuoys.—Forty-eight, with beckets, were supplied, of pattern approved by the Board of Trade. They were placed about the ship.

Lifebelts.—3,560 lifebelts, of the latest improved overhead pattern approved by the Board of Trade, were supplied and placed on board the vessel, and there inspected by the Board of Trade. These were distributed throughout all the sleeping accommodation.

Lifeboats.—Twenty boats in all were fitted on the vessel, and were of the following dimensions and capacities:—

> 14 wood lifeboats, each 30 ft. long by 9 ft. 1 in. broad by 4 ft. deep, with a cubic capacity of 655·2 cubic ft., constructed to carry 65 persons each.
>
> 1 wood cutter, 25 ft. 2 in. long by 7 ft. 2 in. broad by 3 ft. deep, with a cubic capacity of 326·6 cubic ft., constructed to carry 40 persons. } Emergency boats.
>
> 1 wood cutter, 25 ft. 2 in. long by 7 ft. 1 in. broad by 3 ft. deep, with a cubic capacity of 322·1 cubic ft., constructed to carry 40 persons.
>
> 4 Engelhardt collapsible boats, 27 ft. 5 in. long by 8 ft. broad by 3 ft. deep, with a cubic capacity of 376·6 cubic ft., constructed to carry 47 persons each.
>
> Or a total of 11327·9 cubic ft. for 1,178 persons.

The lifeboats and cutters were constructed as follows:—

> The keels were of elm. The stems and stern posts were of oak. They were all clinker built of yellow pine, double fastened with copper nails, clinched over rooves. The timbers were of elm, spaced about 9 in. apart, and the seats pitch pine secured with galvanized iron double knees. The buoyancy tanks in the lifeboats were of 18 oz. copper, and of capacity to meet the Board of Trade requirements.

The lifeboats were fitted with Murray's disengaging gear with arrangements for simultaneously freeing both ends if required. The gear was fastened at a suitable distance from the forward and after ends of the boats, to suit the davits. Life-lines were fitted round the gunwales of the lifeboats. The davit blocks were treble for the lifeboats and double for the cutters. They were of elm, with lignum vitæ roller sheaves, and were bound inside with iron, and had swivel eyes. There were manilla rope falls of sufficient length for lowering the boats to the vessel's light draft, and when the boats were lowered, to be able to reach to the boat winches on the Boat deck.

The lifeboats were stowed on hinged wood chocks on the Boat deck, by groups of three at the forward, and four at the after ends. On each side of the Boat deck the cutters were arranged forward of the group of three and fitted to lash outboard as emergency boats. They were immediately abaft the navigating bridge.

The Engelhardt collapsible lifeboats were stowed abreast of the cutters, one on each side of the ship, and the remaining two on top of the officers' house, immediately abaft the navigating bridge.

The boat equipment was in accordance with the Board of Trade requirements. Sails for each lifeboat and cutter were supplied and stowed in painted bags. Covers were supplied for the lifeboats and cutters, and a sea anchor for each boat. Every lifeboat was furnished with a special spirit boat compass and fitting for holding it; these compasses were carried in a locker on the Boat deck. A provision tank and water beaker were supplied to each boat.

Compasses.—Compasses were supplied as follows :—

> One Kelvin standard compass, with azimuth mirror on compass platform.
>
> One Kelvin steering compass inside of wheel house.
>
> One Kelvin steering compass on captain's bridge.
>
> One light card compass for docking bridge.
>
> Fourteen spirit compasses for lifeboats.

All the ships' compasses were lighted with oil and electric lamps. They were adjusted by Messrs. C. J. Smith, of Southampton, on the passage from Belfast to Southampton and Southampton to Queenstown.

Charts.—All the necessary charts were supplied.

Distress signals.—These were supplied of number and pattern approved by Board of Trade—*i.e.*, 36 socket signals in lieu of guns, 12 ordinary rockets, 2 Manwell Holmes deck flares, 12 blue lights, and 6 lifebuoy lights.

Pumping Arrangements.

The general arrangement of piping was designed so that it was possible to pump from any flooded compartment by two independent systems of 10 in. mains having cross connections between them. These were controlled from above by rods and wheels led to the level of the bulkhead deck. By these it was possible to isolate any flooded space, together with any suctions in it. If any of these should happen accidentally to be left open, and consequently out of reach, it could be shut off from the main by the wheel on the bulkhead deck. This arrangement was specially submitted to the Board of Trade and approved by them.

The double bottom of the vessel was divided by 17 transverse watertight divisions, including those bounding the fore and aft peaks, and again sub-divided by a centre fore and aft bulkhead, and two longitudinal bulkheads, into 46 compartments. Fourteen of these compartments had 8 in. suctions, 23 had 6 in. suctions, and three had 5 in. suctions connected to the 10 in. ballast main suction; six compartments were used exclusively for fresh water.

The following bilge suctions were provided for dealing with water above the double bottom, viz., in No. 1 hold two $3\frac{1}{2}$ in. suctions, No. 2 hold two $3\frac{1}{2}$ in. and two 3 in. suctions, bunker hold two $3\frac{1}{2}$ in. and two 3 in. suctions.

The valves in connection with the forward bilge and ballast suctions were placed in the firemen's passage, the watertight pipe tunnel extending from No. 6 boiler room to the after end of No. 1 hold. In this tunnel, in addition to two 3 in. bilge suctions, one at each end, there was a special $3\frac{1}{2}$ in. suction with valve rod led up to the lower deck above the load line, so as always to have been accessible should the tunnel be flooded accidentally.

In No. 6 boiler room there were three $3\frac{1}{2}$ in., one $4\frac{1}{2}$ in., and two 3 in. suctions.
In No. 5 boiler room there were three $3\frac{1}{2}$ in., one 5 in., and two 3 in. suctions.
In No. 4 boiler room there were three $3\frac{1}{2}$ in., one $4\frac{1}{2}$ in., and two 3 in. suctions.
In No. 3 boiler room there were three $3\frac{1}{2}$ in., one 5 in., and two 3 in. suctions.
In No. 2 boiler room there were three $3\frac{1}{2}$ in., one 5 in., and two 3 in. suctions.
In No. 1 boiler room there were two $3\frac{1}{2}$ in., one 5 in., and two 3 in. suctions.
In the reciprocating engine room there were two $3\frac{1}{2}$ in., six 3 in., two 18 in., and two 5 in. suctions.
In the turbine engine room there were two $3\frac{1}{2}$ in., three 3 in., two 18 in., two 5 in., and one 4 in. suctions.
In the electric engine room there were four $3\frac{1}{2}$ in. suctions.
In the store rooms above the electric engine room there was one 3 in. suction.
In the forward tunnel compartment there were two $3\frac{1}{2}$ in. suctions.
In the watertight flat over the tunnel compartment there were two 3 in. suctions.
In the tunnel after compartment there were two $3\frac{1}{2}$ in. suctions.
In the watertight flat over the tunnel after compartment there were two 3 in. suctions.

Electrical Installation.

Main Generating Sets.—There were four engines and dynamos, each having a capacity of 400 kilowatts at 100 volts, and consisting of a vertical three-crank compound-forced lubrication enclosed engine, of sufficient power to drive the electrical plant.

The engines were direct-coupled to their respective dynamos.

These four main sets were situated in a separate watertight compartment about 63 ft. long by 24 ft. high, adjoining the after end of the turbine room at the level of the inner bottom.

Steam to the electric engines was supplied from two separate lengths of steam pipes, connecting on the port side to the five single-ended boilers in compartment No. 1 and two in compartment No. 2, and on the starboard side to the auxiliary steam pipe which derived steam from the five single-ended boilers in No. 1 compartment, two in No. 2, and two in No. 4.   By connections at the engine room forward bulkhead steam could be taken from any boiler in the ship.

Auxiliary Generating Sets.—In addition to the four main generating sets, there were two 30 kilowatt engines and dynamos situated on a platform in the turbine engine room casing on saloon deck level, 20 ft. above the water line.   They were of the same general type as the main sets.

These auxiliary emergency sets were connected to the boilers by means of a separate steam pipe running along the working passage above E deck, with branches from three boiler rooms, Nos. 2, 3 and 5, so that should the main sets be temporarily out of action the auxiliary sets could provide current for such lights and power appliances as would be required in the event of emergency.

Electric Lighting.—The total number of incandescent lights was 10,000, ranging from 16 to 100 candle power, the majority being of Tantallum type, except in the cargo spaces and for the portable fittings, where carbon lamps were provided. Special dimming lamps of small amount of light were provided in the first-class rooms.

Electric Heating and Power and Mechanical Ventilation.—Altogether 562 electric heaters and 153 electric motors were installed throughout the vessel, including six 50-cwt. and two 30-cwt. cranes, four 3-ton cargo winches, and four 15-cwt. boat winches.

There were also four electric passenger lifts, three forward of the first-class main entrance and one in the second-class forward entrance, each to carry twelve persons.

Telephones.—Loud speaking telephones of navy pattern were fitted for communication between the following :—

> Wheel house on the navigating bridge and the forecastle.
> Wheel house on the navigating bridge and the look-out station on the crow's nest.
> Wheel house on the navigating bridge and the engine room.
> Wheel house on the navigating bridge and the poop.
> Chief engineer's cabin and the engine room.
> Engine room and Nos. 1, 2, 3, 4, 5 and 6 stokeholds.

These were operated both from the ship's lighting circuit, through a motor generator, and alternatively by a stand-by battery, which by means of an automatic switch could be introduced in the circuit should the main supply fail.

There was also a separate telephone system for intercommunication between a number of the chief officials and service rooms, through a 50-line exchange switchboard.

A number of the pantries and galleys were also in direct telephonic communication.

Wireless Telegraphy.—The wireless telegraphy system was worked by a Marconi 5 kilowatt motor generator.   The house for the Marconi instruments was situated on the Boat deck close to the bridge   There were four parallel aerial wires extended between the masts, fastened to light booms; from the aerials the connecting wires were led to the instruments in the house.   There were two complete sets of apparatus, one for the transmitting and one for receiving messages, the former being placed in a sound-proof chamber in one corner of the wireless house.

There was also an independent storage battery and coil, in event of the failure of the current supply, which came from the ship's dynamos.

Submarine signalling.—The Submarine Signal Company's apparatus was provided for receiving signals from the submarine bells.   Small tanks containing the microphones were placed on the inside of the hull of the vessel on the port and starboard sides below the water level, and were connected by wires to receivers situated in the navigating room on the port side of the officer's deck-house.

Various.—The whistles were electrically actuated on the Willett Bruce system.   The boiler room telegraphs, stoking indicators, rudder indicators, clocks and thermostats were also electrical.   The watertight doors were released by electric magnets.

Emergency Circuit.—A separate and distinct installation was fitted in all parts of the vessel, deriving current from the two 30 kilowatt sets above mentioned, so that in the event of the current from the main dynamos being unavailable an independent supply was obtainable. Connected to the emergency circuit were above 500 incandescent lamps fitted throughout all passenger, crew and machinery compartments, at the end of passages, and near stairways, also on the Boat deck, to enable anyone to find their way from one part of the ship to the other.

The following were also connected to the emergency circuit by means of change-over switches:—Five arc lamps, seven cargo and gangway lanterns, Marconi apparatus, mast, side and stern lights, and all lights on bridge, including those for captain's, navigating and chart rooms, wheelhouse, telegraphs and Morse signalling lanterns, and four electrically-driven boat winches. These latter, situated on the boat deck, were each capable of lifting a load of 15 cwt. at a speed of 100 ft. per minute.

Ventilating.—There were 12 electrically driven fans for supplying air to the stokeholds; six electrically driven fans for engine and turbine room ventilation. There were fans for engine and boiler rooms.

Machinery.

Description.—The propelling machinery was of the combination type, having two sets of reciprocating engines driving the wing propellers, and a low-pressure turbine working the centre propeller. Steam was supplied by 24 double-ended boilers, and five single-ended boilers, arranged for a working pressure of 215 lb. per square inch. The turbine was placed in a separate compartment aft of the reciprocating engine-room and divided from it by a watertight bulkhead. The main condensers, with their circulating pumps and air pumps, were placed in the turbine room. The boilers were arranged in six watertight compartments, the single-ended boilers being placed in the one nearest the main engines, the whole being built under Board of Trade survey for passenger certificate.

Reciprocating Engines.—The reciprocating engines were of the four-crank triple expansion type. Each set had four inverted, direct-acting cylinders, the high-pressure having a diameter of 54 in., the intermediate pressure of 84 in., and each of the two low-pressure cylinders of 97 in., all with a stroke of 6 ft. 3 in. The valves of the high pressure and intermediate cylinders were of the piston type, and the low-pressure cylinder had double-ported slide valves, fitted with Stephenson link motion. Each engine was reversed by a Brown's type of direct-acting steam and hydraulic engine. There was also a separate steam-driven high-pressure pump fitted for operating cither or both of the reversing engines. This alternative arrangement was a stand-by in case of breakdown of the steam pipes to these engines.

Turbine.—The low-pressure turbine was of the Parson's reaction type, direct coupled to the centre line of shafting and arranged for driving in the ahead direction only. It exhausted to the two condensers, placed one on each side of it. A shut-off valve was fitted in each of the eduction pipes leading to the condensers. An emergency governor was fitted and arranged to shut off steam to the turbine and simultaneously change over the exhaust from the reciprocating engines to the condensers, should the speed of the turbine become excessive through the breaking of a shaft or other accident.

Boilers.—All the boilers were 15 ft. 9 in. in diameter, the 24 double-ended boilers being 20 ft. long, and the single-ended 11 ft. 9 in. long. Each double-ended boiler had six, and each single-ended boiler three furnaces, with a total heating surface of 144,142 sq. ft. and a grate surface of 3,466 sq. ft. The boilers were constructed in accordance with the rules of the Board of Trade for a working pressure of 215 lb. per square inch. They were arranged for working under natural draught, assisted by fans, which blew air into the open stokehold.

Auxiliary Steam Pipes.—The five single-ended boilers and those in boiler-rooms Nos. 2 and 4 had separate steam connections to the pipe supplying steam for working the auxiliary machinery, and the five single-ended boilers and the two port boilers in boiler room No. 2 had separate steam connections to the pipe supplying steam for working the electric light engines. A cross connection was also made between the main and auxiliary pipes in the reciprocating engine-room, so that the auxiliaries could be worked from any boiler in the ship. Steam pipes also were led separately from three of the boiler-rooms (Nos. 2, 3, 5) above the watertight bulkheads and along the working passage to the emergency electric light engines placed above the load-line in the turbine room.   Pipes were also led from this steam supply to the pumps in the engine room, which were connected to the bilges throughout the ship.

Main Steam Pipes.—There were two main lines of steam pipes led to the engine room, with shut-off valves at three of the bulkheads.   Besides the shut-off valves at the engine room bulkhead, a quick-acting emergency valve was fitted on each main steam pipe, so that the steam could at once be shut-off in case of rupture of the main pipe.

Condensing Plant and Pumps.—There were two main condensers, having a combined cooling surface of 50,550 square feet, designed to work under a vacuum of 28 ins. with cooling water at 60 deg. Fahr.   The condensers were pear-shaped in section, and built of mild steel plates.

Four gunmetal centrifugal pumps were fitted for circulating water through the condensers.   Each pump had suction and discharge pipes of 29 in. bore, and was driven by a compound engine.   Besides the main sea suctions, two of the pumps had direct bilge suctions from the turbine room and the other two from the reciprocating engine room.   The bilge suctions were 18 in. diameter.   Four of Weir's "Dual" air pumps were fitted, two to each condenser, and discharged to two feed-tanks placed in the turbine engine room.

Bilge and Ballast Pumps.—The ship was also fitted with the following pumps : Five ballast and bilge pumps, each capable of discharging 250 tons of water per hour; three bilge pumps, each of 150 tons per hour capacity.

One ash ejector was placed in each of the large boiler compartments to work the ash ejectors, and to circulate or feed the boilers as required.   This pump was also connected to the bilges, except in the case of three of the boiler rooms, where three of the ballast and bilge pumps were placed.   The pumps in each case had direct bilge suctions as well as a connection to the main bilge pipe, so that each boiler room might be independent.   The remainder of the auxiliary pumps were placed in the reciprocating and turbine engine rooms.   Two ballast pumps were placed in the reciprocating engine room, with large suctions from the bilges direct and from the bilge main.   Two bilge pumps were also arranged to draw from bilges.   One bilge pump was placed in the turbine room and one of the hot salt-water pumps had a connection from the bilge main pipe for use in emergency. A 10 in. main ballast pipe was carried fore and aft through the ship with separate connections to each tank, and with filling pipes from the sea connected at intervals for trimming purposes.   The five ballast pumps were arranged to draw from this pipe.   A double line of bilge main pipe was fitted forward of No. 5 boiler room and aft of No. 1.

General.

There were four elliptical-shaped funnels; the three forward ones took the waste gases from the boiler furnaces, and the after one was placed over the turbine hatch and was used as a ventilator.   The galley funnels were led up this funnel.   The uptakes by which the waste gases were conveyed to the funnels were united immediately above the watertight bulkhead which separated the boiler rooms.

All overhead discharge from the circulating pumps, ballast pumps, bilge pumps, etc., were below the deep load-line, but above the light line.

The boilers were supported in built steel cradles, and were stayed to the ship's side and to each other athwart ships by strong steel stays.   Built steel chocks were also fitted to prevent movement fore and aft.

Silent blow-offs from the main steam pipes were connected direct to both condensers.

Crew and Passengers.

When the "Titanic" left Queenstown on 11th April the total number of persons employed on board in any capacity was 885.
The respective ratings of these persons were as follows:—

> Deck Department   ...   66
> Engine Department   ...   325
> Victualling Department   494
>   ——— 885

Eight bandsmen were included in the second-class passenger list.

In the Deck Department the

Master, Edward Charles Smith, held an Extra Master's Certificate.
Chief Officer H. F. Wilde held an Ordinary Master's Certificate.
1st Officer W. M. Murdoch held an Ordinary Master's Certificate.
2nd Officer C. H. Lightoller held an Extra Master's Certificate.
3rd Officer H. J. Pitman held an Ordinary Master's Certificate.
4th Officer J. G. Boxall held an Extra Master's Certificate.
5th Officer H. G. Lowe held an Ordinary Master's Certificate.
6th Officer J. P. Moody held an Ordinary Master's Certificate.

In the Engine Department were included the Chief Engineer and 7 senior and 17 assistant engineers.

In the Victualling Department there were 23 women employed.

The total number of passengers on board was 1,316.

	Male.	Female.	Total.
Of these 1st class	180	145	325
2nd class	179	106	285
3rd class	510	196	706
			—— 1,316

Of the above 6 children were in the 1st class.
24   ,,   ,,   2nd class.
79   ,,   ,,   3rd class.
———
or 109 in all.

About 410 of the 3rd class passengers were foreigners, and these, with the foreigners in the 1st and 2nd class and in the Victualling Department would make a total of nearly 500 persons on board who were presumably not English speaking, so far as it is possible to ascertain. The disposition of the different classes of passengers and of the crew in the ship has already been described (pp. 10-15). In all 2,201 persons were on board.

2.—ACCOUNT OF THE SHIP'S JOURNEY ACROSS THE ATLANTIC, THE MESSAGES SHE RECEIVED AND THE DISASTER.

The Sailing Orders.

The masters of vessels belonging to the White Star Line are not given any special "sailing orders" before the commencement of any particular voyage. It is understood, however, that the "tracks" or "lane routes" proper to the particular time of the year, and agreed upon by the great steamship companies, are to be generally adhered to. Should any master see fit during this passage to deviate from his route he has to report on and explain this deviation at the end of his voyage. When such deviation has been in the interests of safety, and not merely to shorten his passage, his action has always been approved of by the Company.

A book of "General Ship's Rules and Uniform Regulations" is also issued by the Company as a guide; there are in this book no special instructions in regard to ice, but there is a general instruction that the safety of the lives of the passengers and ship are to be the first consideration.

Besides the book of Ship's Rules, every master when first appointed to command a ship is addressed by special letter from the Company, of which the following passage is an extract:—"You are to dismiss all idea of competitive passages with other vessels and to concentrate your attention upon a cautious, prudent and ever watchful system of navigation, which shall lose time or suffer any other temporary inconvenience rather than incur the slightest risk which can be avoided." Mr. Sanderson, one of the directors, in his evidence says with reference to the above letter:—"We never fail to tell them in handing them these letters that we do not wish them to take it as a mere matter of form; that we wish them to read these letters, and to write an acknowledgment to us that they have read them, and that they will be influenced by what we have said in those letters."

Margin references: Ismay 18625; 18614; 18615; 18618; 18612; 18613; 18611; 18629; Sanderson 19271

The Route followed.

The "Titanic" left Southampton on Wednesday, 10th April, and, after calling at Cherbourg, proceeded to Queenstown, from which port she sailed on the afternoon of Thursday, 11th April, following what was at that time the accepted outward-bound route for mail steamers from the Fastnet Light, off the south-west coast of Ireland, to the Nantucket Shoal light vessel, off the coast of the United States. It is desirable here to explain that it has been, since 1899, the practice, by common agreement between the great North Atlantic steamship companies, to follow lane routes, to be used by their ships at the different seasons of the year. Speaking generally, it may be said that the selection of these routes has hitherto been based on the importance of avoiding as much as possible the areas where fog and ice are prevalent at certain seasons, without thereby unduly lengthening the passage across the Atlantic; and also with the view of keeping the tracks of "outward" and "homeward" bound mail steamers well clear of one another. A further advantage is that, in case of a breakdown, vessels are likely to receive timely assistance from other vessels following the same route. The decisions arrived at by the steamship companies referred to above have, from time to time, been communicated to the Hydrographic Office, and the routes have there been marked on the North Atlantic route charts printed and published by the Admiralty; and they have also been embodied in the Sailing Directions.

Before the "Titanic" disaster the accepted mail steamers outward track between January 15th and August 14th followed the arc of a great circle between the Fastnet Light and a point in latitude 42° N. and 47° W. (sometimes termed the "turning point"), and from thence by Rhumb Line so as to pass just south of the Nantucket Shoal light vessel, and from this point on to New York. This track, usually called the Outward Southern Track, was that followed by the "Titanic" on her journey.

An examination of the North Atlantic route chart shows that this track passes about 25 miles south (that is outside) of the edge of the area marked "field ice between March and July," but from 100 to 300 miles to the northward (that is inside) of the dotted line on the chart marked, "Icebergs have been seen within this line in April, May and June."

That is to say, assuming the areas indicated to be based on the experience of many years, this track might be taken as passing clear of field ice under the usual conditions of that time of year, but well inside the area in which icebergs might be seen.

It is instructive here to remark that had the " turning point " been in long. 45° W. and lat. 38° N., that is some 240 miles to the south-eastward, the total distance of the passage would only have been increased by about 220 miles, or some 10 hours' steaming for a 22-knot ship. This is the route which was provisionally decided on by the great Transatlantic companies subsequent to the " Titanic " disaster.

It must not be supposed that the lane routes referred to had never been changed before. Owing to the presence of ice in 1903, 1904 and 1905 from about early in April to mid-June or early in July, westward-board vessels crossed the meridian of 47° W. in lat. 41° N., that is 60 miles further south than the then accepted track.

The publications known as " Sailing Directions," compiled by the Hydrographic Office at the Admiralty, indicate the caution which it is necessary to use in regions where ice is likely to be found.

The following is an extract from one of these books, named " United States Pilot (East Coast)," part I. (second edition, 1909, page 34), referring to the ocean passages of the large Transatlantic mail and passenger steamers :—

" To these vessels, one of the chief dangers in crossing the Atlantic " lies in the probability of encountering masses of ice, both in the form of " bergs and of extensive fields of solid compact ice, released at the breaking " up of winter in the Arctic regions, and drifted down by the Labrador " Current across their direct route. Ice is more likely to be encountered " in this route between April and August, both months inclusive, than at " other times, although icebergs have been seen at all seasons northward " of the parallel of 43° N., but not often so far south after August.

" These icebergs are sometimes over 200 ft. in height and of con- " siderable extent. They have been seen as far south as lat. 39° N., " to obtain which position they must have crossed the Gulf Stream " impelled by the cold Arctic current underrunning the warm waters of " the Gulf Stream. That this should happen is not to be wondered at " when it is considered that the specific gravity of fresh-water ice, of " which these bergs are composed, is about seven-eighths that of sea water; " so that, however vast the berg may appear to the eye of the observer, he " can in reality see one-eighth of its bulk, the remaining seven-eighths " being submerged and subject to the deep-water currents of the ocean. " The track of an iceberg is indeed directed mainly by current, so small " a portion of its surface being exposed to the action of the winds that its " course is but slightly retarded or deflected by moderate breezes. On the " Great Bank of Newfoundland bergs are often observed to be moving " south or south-east; those that drift westward of Cape Race usually " pass between Green and St. Pierre Banks.

" The route chart of the North Atlantic, No. 2058, shows the limits " within which both field ice and icebergs may be met with, and where it " should be carefully looked out for at all times, but especially during the " spring and summer seasons. From this chart it would appear that " whilst the southern and eastern limits of field ice are about lat. 42° N. " and long. 45° W., icebergs may be met with much farther from New- " foundland; in April, May and June they have been seen as far South as " lat. 39° N., and as far east as long. 38° 30' W."

And again on page 35:—

" It is, in fact, impossible to give, within the outer limits named, any " distinct idea of where ice may be expected, and no rule can be laid down " to ensure safe navigation, as its position and the quantity met with differs " so greatly in different seasons. Everything must depend upon the vigi- " lance, caution and skill with which a vessel is navigated when crossing " the dangerous ice-bearing regions of the Atlantic Ocean."

Similar warnings as to ice are also given in the " Nova Scotia (South-East Coast) and Bay of Fundy Pilot " (sixth edition, 1911) which is also published by the Hydrographic Office.

Both the above quoted books were supplied to the master of the "Titanic" (together with other necessary charts and books) before that ship left Southampton.

The above extracts show that it is quite incorrect to assume that icebergs had never before been encountered or field ice observed so far south, at the particular time of year when the "Titanic" disaster occurred; but it is true to say that the field ice was certainly at that time further south than it has been seen for many years.

It may be useful here to give some definitions of the various forms of ice to be met with in these latitudes, although there is frequently some confusion in their use.

An Iceberg may be defined as a detached portion of a Polar glacier carried out to sea. The ice of an iceberg formed from a glacier is of quite fresh water, only about an eighth of its mass floats above the surface of sea water.

A "Growler" is a colloquial term applied to icebergs of small mass, which therefore only show a small portion above the surface. It is not infrequently a berg which has turned over, and is therefore showing what has been termed "black ice," or more correctly, dark blue ice.

Pack Ice is the floating ice which covers wide areas of the Polar seas, broken into large pieces, which are driven ("packed") together by wind and current, so as to form a practically continuous sheet. Such ice is generally frozen from sea water, and not derived from glaciers.

Field Ice is a term usually applied to frozen sea water floating in much looser form than pack ice.

An Icefloe is the term generally applied to the same ice (*i.e.*, field ice) in a smaller quantity.

A Floe Berg is a stratified mass of floe ice (*i.e.*, sea-water ice).

Ice Messages Received.

The "Titanic" followed the Outward Southern Track until Sunday, the 14th April, in the usual way. At 11.40 p.m. on that day she struck an iceberg and at 2.20 a.m. on the next day she foundered.

At 9 a.m. ("Titanic" time) on that day a wireless message from the s.s. "Caronia" was received by Captain Smith. It was as follows:—

Turnbull, 16199

"Captain, 'Titanic.'—West-bound steamers report bergs growlers "and field ice in 42° N. from 49° to 51° W., 12th April. Compli- "ments.—Barr."

It will be noticed that this message referred to bergs, growlers and field ice sighted on the 12th April—at least 48 hours before the time of the collision. At the time this message was received the "Titanic's" position was about lat. 43° 35' N. and long. 43° 50' W. Captain Smith acknowledged the receipt of this message.

At 1.42 p.m. a wireless message from the s.s. "Baltic" was received by Captain Smith. It was as follows:—

16176

"Captain Smith, 'Titanic.'—Have had moderate, variable winds and "clear, fine weather since leaving. Greek steamer 'Athenai' reports "passing icebergs and large quantities of field ice to-day in lat. 41° 51' "N., long. 49° 52' W. Last night we spoke German oiltank steamer "'Deutschland,' Stettin to Philadelphia, not under control, short of coal, "lat. 40° 42' N., long. 55° 11' W. Wishes to be reported to New York "and other steamers. Wish you and 'Titanic' all success.—Commander."

At the time this message was received the "Titanic" position was about 42° 35' N., 45° 50' W. Captain Smith acknowledged the receipt of this message also.

Mr. Ismay, the Managing Director of the White Star Line, was on board the "Titanic," and it appears that the Master handed the Baltic's message to Mr. Ismay almost immediately after it was received. This no doubt was in order that Mr. Ismay might know that ice was to be expected. Mr. Ismay states that he understood from the message that they would get up to the ice "that night." Mr. Ismay showed this message to two ladies, and it is therefore probable that many persons on board became aware of its contents. This message ought in my opinion to have been put on the board in the chart room as soon as it was received. It remained, however, in Mr. Ismay's possession until 7.15 p.m., when the Master asked Mr. Ismay to return it. It was then that it was first posted in the chart room.

This was considerably before the time at which the vessel reached the position recorded in the message. Nevertheless, I think it was irregular for the Master to part with the document, and improper for Mr. Ismay to retain it, but the incident had, in my opinion, no connection with or influence upon the manner in which the vessel was navigated by the Master.

It appears that about 1.45 p.m. ("Titanic" time) on the 14th a message was sent from the German steamer "Amerika" to the Hydrographic Office in Washington, which was in the following terms :—

> "'Amerika' passed two large icebergs in 41° 27' N., 50° 8' W., on 16122
> "the 14th April."

This was a position south of the point of the "Titanic's" disaster. The message does not mention at what hour the bergs had been observed. It was a private message for the Hydrographer at Washington, but it passed to the "Titanic" because she was nearest to Cape Race, to which station it had to be sent in order to reach Washington. Being a message affecting navigation, it should in the ordinary course have been taken to the bridge. So far as can be ascertained, it was never heard of by anyone on board the "Titanic" outside the Marconi room. There were two Marconi operators in the Marconi room, namely, Phillips, who perished, and Bride, who survived and gave evidence. Bride did not receive the "Amerika" message nor did Phillips mention it to him, though the two had much conversation together after it had been received. I am of opinion that when this message reached the Marconi room it was put aside by Phillips to wait until the "Titanic" would be within call of Cape Race (at about 8 or 8.30 p.m.), and that it was never handed to any officer of the "Titanic."

At 5.50 p.m. the "Titanic's" course (which had been S. 62° W.) was Boxall, 15315 changed to bring her on a westerly course for New York. In ordinary circumstances this change in her course should have been made about half an hour earlier, but she seems on this occasion to have continued for about ten miles longer on her south-westerly course before turning, with the result that she found herself, after altering course at 5.50 p.m. about four or five miles south of the customary route on a course S. 86° W. true. Her course, as thus set, would bring her at the time of the collision to a point about two miles to the southward of the customary route and four miles south and considerably to the westward of the indicated position of the "Baltic's" ice. Her position at the time of the collision would also be well to the southward of the indicated position of the ice mentioned in the "Caronia" message. This change of course was so insignificant that in my opinion it cannot have been made in consequence of information as to ice.

In this state of things, at 7.30 p.m. a fourth message was received, and is said by the Marconi operator Bride to have been delivered to the bridge. This message was from the s.s. "Californian" to the s.s. "Antillian," but was picked up by the "Titanic." It was as follows :—

> "To Captain, 'Antillian,' 6.30 p.m. apparent ship's time; lat. Evans, 8943
> "42° 3' N., long. 49° 9' W. Three large bergs five miles to southward of
> "us. Regards.—Lord."

Bride does not remember to what officer he delivered this message.

By the time the "Titanic" reached the position of the collision (11.40 p.m.) she had gone about 50 miles to the westward of the indicated position of the ice mentioned in this fourth message. Thus it would appear that before the collision she had gone clear of the indicated positions of ice contained in the messages from the "Baltic" and "Californian." As to the ice advised by the "Caronia" message, so far as it consisted of small bergs and field ice, it had before the time of the collision possibly drifted with the Gulf Stream to the eastward; and so far as it consisted of large bergs (which would be deep enough in the water to reach the Labrador current) it had probably gone to the southward. It was urged by Sir Robert Finlay, who appeared for the owners, that this is strong evidence that the "Titanic" had been carefully and successfully navigated so as to avoid the ice of which she had received warning. Mr. Ismay, however, stated that he understood Ismay, 18461 from the "Baltic" message that "we would get up to the ice that night."

There was a fifth message received in the Marconi room of the "Titanic"

Turnbull,
16221 at 9.40 p.m.   This was from a steamer called the "Mesaba."   It was in the
following terms :—

> "From 'Mesaba' to 'Titanic' and all east-bound ships.   Ice report
> "in lat. 42° N. to 41° 25′ N., long. 49° to long. 50° 30′ W.   Saw much
> "heavy pack ice and great number large icebergs.   Also field ice.   Weather
> "good, clear."

This message clearly indicated the presence of ice in the immediate vicinity
of the "Titanic," and if it had reached the bridge would perhaps have affected
the navigation of the vessel.   Unfortunately, it does not appear to have been
delivered to the Master or to any of the officers.   The Marconi operator was very busy
from 8 o'clock onward transmitting messages via Cape Race for passengers on board
the "Titanic," and the probability is that he failed to grasp the significance and
importance of the message, and put it aside until he should be less busy.   It was
never acknowledged by Captain Smith, and I am satisfied that it was not received
by him.   But, assuming Sir Robert Finlay's contentions to be well founded that the
"Titanic" had been navigated so as to avoid the "Baltic" and the "Californian"
ice, and that the "Caronia" ice had drifted to the eastward and to the southward,
still there can be no doubt, if the evidence of Mr. Lightoller, the second officer, is
to be believed, that both he and the Master knew that the danger of meeting
ice still existed.   Mr. Lightoller says that the Master showed him the
"Caronia" message about 12.45 p.m. on the 14th April when he was on the
bridge.   He was about to go off watch, and he says he made a rough calculation
Lightoller,
13537, 13556 in his head which satisfied him that the "Titanic" would not reach the position
mentioned in the message until he came on watch again at 6 p.m.   At 6 p.m.
Mr. Lightoller came on the bridge again to take over the ship from Mr. Wilde,
the chief officer, (dead).   He does not remember being told anything about the
"Baltic" message, which had been received at 1.42 p.m.   Mr. Lightoller then
requested Mr. Moody, the sixth officer, (dead), to let him know "at what time we
"should reach the vicinity of ice," and says that he thinks Mr. Moody reported
"about 11 o'clock."   Mr. Lightoller says that 11 o'clock did not agree with a mental
calculation he himself had made and which showed 9.30 as the time.   This mental
calculation he at first said he had made before Mr. Moody gave him 11 o'clock as
the time, but later on he corrected this, and said his mental calculation was made
between 7 and 8 o'clock, and after Mr. Moody had mentioned 11.   He did not point
out the difference to him, and thought that perhaps Mr. Moody had made his
calculations on the basis of some "other" message.   Mr. Lightoller excuses himself
for not pointing out the difference by saying that Mr. Moody was busy at the time,
probably with stellar observations.   It is, however, an odd circumstance that Mr.
Lightoller, who believed that the vicinity of ice would be reached before his watch
ended at 10 p.m., should not have mentioned the fact to Mr. Moody, and it is also
odd that if he thought that Mr. Moody was working on the basis of some "other"
message, he did not ask what the other message was or where it came from.   The
point, however, of Mr. Lightoller's evidence is that they both thought that the
vicinity of ice would be reached before midnight.   When he was examined as to
whether he did not fear that on entering the indicated ice region he might run foul
of a growler (a low-lying berg) he answers : "No, I judged I should see it with
"sufficient distinctness" and at a distance of a "mile and a half, more probably
13569 "two miles."   He then adds : "In the event of meeting ice there are many things
"we look for.   In the first place, a slight breeze.   Of course, the stronger the breeze
"the more visible will the ice be, or, rather, the breakers on the ice."   He is then
asked whether there was any breeze on this night, and he answers : "When I left
"the deck at 10 o'clock there was a slight breeze.   Oh, pardon me, no; I take that
"back.   No, it was calm, perfectly calm," and almost immediately afterwards he
describes the sea as "absolutely flat."   It appeared, according to this witness, that
about 9 o'clock the Master came on the bridge and that Mr. Lightoller had a
conversation with him which lasted half an hour.   This conversation, so far as it is
material, is described by Mr. Lightoller in the following words : "We commenced
"to speak about the weather.   He said, 'there is not much wind.'   I said, 'No, it
"'is a flat calm,' as a matter of fact.   He repeated it, he said, 'A flat calm.'   I said,
"'Quite flat; there is no wind.'   I said something about it was rather a pity the
"breeze had not kept up whilst we were going through the ice region.   Of course,
"my reason was obvious; he knew I meant the water ripples breaking on the base
"of the berg. . . .   We then discussed the indications of ice.   I remember
"saying 'In any case, there will be a certain amount of reflected light from the

" 'bergs.' He said, ' Oh, yes, there will be a certain amount of reflected light.' I
" said or he said—blue was said between us—that even though the blue side of the
" berg was towards us, probably the outline, the white outline, would give us suffi-
" cient warning, that we should be able to see it at a good distance, and as far as we
" could see, we should be able to see it. Of course, it was just with regard to that
" possibility of the blue side being towards us, and that if it did happen to be
" turned with the purely blue side towards us, there would still be the white outline."
Further on Mr. Lightoller says that he told the Master nothing about his own
calculation as to coming up with the ice at 9.30 or about Mr. Moody's calculation as
to coming up with it at 11.

 The conversation with the Master ended with the Master saying, " If it
" becomes at all doubtful let me know at once; I will be just inside." This remark 13635
Mr. Lightoller says undoubtedly referred to ice. 13653

 At 9.30 the Master went to his room, and the first thing that Mr. Lightoller
did afterwards was to send a message to the crow's nest " to keep a sharp look-out 13657
" for ice, particularly small ice and growlers," until daylight. There seems to be no
doubt that this message was in fact sent, and that it was passed on to the next look-
outs when they came on watch. Hitchins, the quartermaster, says he heard Mr.
Lightoller give the message to Mr. Moody, and both the men in the crow's nest at
the time (Jewell and Symons) speak to having received it. From 9.30 to 10 o'clock,
when his watch ended, Mr. Lightoller remained on the bridge " looking out for
" ice." He also said that the night order book for the 14th had a footnote about
keeping a sharp look-out for ice, and that this note was " initialled by every 13700
" officer." At 10 o'clock Mr. Lightoller handed over the watch to Mr. Murdoch,
the first officer, (dead), telling him that " we might be up around the ice any time
" now." That Mr. Murdoch knew of the danger of meeting ice appears from the
evidence of Hemming, a lamp trimmer, who says that about 7.15 p.m. Mr. Murdoch Hemming,
told him to go forward and see the forescuttle hatch closed, " as we are in the vicinity 17707
" of ice and there is a glow coming from that, and I want everything dark before
" the bridge."

 The foregoing evidence establishes quite clearly that Captain Smith, the
master, Mr. Murdoch, the first officer, Mr. Lightoller, the second officer, and
Mr. Moody, the sixth officer, all knew on the Sunday evening that the vessel was
entering a region where ice might be expected, and this being so, it seems to me to
be of little importance to consider whether the Master had by design or otherwise
succeeded in avoiding the particular ice indicated in the three messages received by
him.

Speed of the Ship.

 The entire passage had been made at high speed, though not at the ship's
maximum, and this speed was never reduced until the collision was unavoidable. Hi'chins 965
At 10 p.m. the ship was registering 45 knots every two hours by the Cherub log.

 The quartermaster on watch aft, when the " Titanic " struck, states that the Rowe, 17607
log, reset at noon, then registered 260 knots, and the fourth officer, when working up
the position from 7.30 p.m. to the time of the collision, states he estimated the
" Titanic's " speed as 22 knots, and this is also borne out by evidence that the engines Boxall 15645
were running continuously at 75 revolutions.

The Weather Conditions.

 From 6 p.m. onwards to the time of the collision the weather was perfectly Lightoller,
clear and fine. There was no moon, the stars were out, and there was not a cloud in 13616
the sky. There was, however, a drop in temperature of 10 deg. in slightly less than
two hours, and by about 7.30 p.m. the temperature was 33 deg. F., and it eventually
fell to 32 deg. F. That this was not necessarily an indication of ice, is borne out
by the Sailing Directions. The Nova Scotia (S.E. Coast) and Bay of Fundy Pilot
(6th edition, 1911, page 16) says :—

  " No reliance can be placed on any warning being conveyed to a
  " mariner by a fall of temperature either of the air or sea, on approaching
  " ice. Some decrease in temperature has occasionally been recorded, but
  " more often none has been observed."

 Sir Ernest Shackleton was, however, of opinion that " if there was no wind Shackleton,
" and the temperature fell abnormally for the time of the year, I would consider 25062
" that I was approaching an area which might have ice in it."

Action that should have been taken.

The question is what ought the Master to have done. I am advised that with the knowledge of the proximity of ice which the Master had, two courses were open to him : The one was to stand well to the southward instead of turning up to a westerly course; the other was to reduce speed materially as night approached. He did neither. The alteration of the course at 5.50 p.m. was so insignificant that it cannot be attributed to any intention to avoid ice. This deviation brought the vessel back to within about two miles of the customary route before 11.30 p.m. And there was certainly no reduction of speed. Why, then, did the Master persevere in his course and maintain his speed? The answer is to be found in the evidence. It was shown that for many years past, indeed, for a quarter of a century or more, the practice of liners using this track when in the vicinity of ice at night had been in clear weather to keep the course, to maintain the speed and to trust to a sharp look-out to enable them to avoid the danger. This practice, it was said, had been justified by experience, no casualties having resulted from it. I accept the evidence as to the practice and as to the immunity from casualties which is said to have accompanied it. But the event has proved the practice to be bad. Its root is probably to be found in competition and in the desire of the public for quick passages rather than in the judgment of navigators. But unfortunately experience appeared to justify it. In these circumstances I am not able to blame Captain Smith. He had not the experience which his own misfortune has afforded to those whom he has left behind, and he was doing only that which other skilled men would have done in the same position. It was suggested at the bar that he was yielding to influences which ought not to have affected him : that the presence of Mr. Ismay on board and the knowledge which he perhaps had of a conversation between Mr. Ismay and the Chief Engineer at Queenstown about the speed of the ship and the consumption of coal probably induced him to neglect precautions which he would otherwise have taken. But I do not believe this. The evidence shows that he was not trying to make any record passage or indeed any exceptionally quick passage. He was not trying to please anybody, but was exercising his own discretion in the way he thought best. He made a mistake, a very grievous mistake, but one in which, in face of the practice and of past experience, negligence cannot be said to have had any part; and in the absence of negligence it is, in my opinion, impossible to fix Captain Smith with blame. It is, however, to be hoped that the last has been heard of the practice and that for the future it will be abandoned for what we now know to be more prudent and wiser measures. What was a mistake in the case of the "Titanic" would without doubt be negligence in any similar case in the future.

The Collision.

Mr. Lightoller turned over the ship to Mr. Murdoch, the first officer, at 10 o'clock, telling him that the ship was within the region where ice had been reported. He also told him of the message he had sent to the crow's nest, and of his conversation with the Master, and of the latter's orders.

The ship appears to have run on, on the same course, until, at a little before 11.40, one of the look-outs in the crow's-nest struck three blows on the gong, which was the accepted warning for something ahead, following this immediately afterwards by a telephone message to the bridge "Iceberg right ahead." Almost simultaneously with the three gong signal Mr. Murdoch, the officer of the watch, gave the order "Hard-a-starboard," and immediately telegraphed down to the engine-room "Stop. Full speed astern," The helm was already "hard over," and the ship's head had fallen off about two points to port, when she collided with an iceberg well forward on her starboard side.

Mr. Murdoch at the same time pulled the lever over which closed the watertight doors in the engine and boiler rooms.

The Master " rushed out " on to the bridge and asked Mr. Murdoch what the ship had struck.

Mr. Murdoch replied : " An iceberg, Sir. I hard-a-starboarded and reversed "the engines, and I was going to hard-a-port round it but she was too close. I could " not do any more. I have closed the watertight doors."

From the evidence given it appears that the "Titanic" had turned about two points to port before the collision occurred. From various experiments subsequently made with the s.s. "Olympic," a sister ship to the "Titanic," it was found that travelling at the same rate as the "Titanic," about 37 seconds would be required

Lightoller,
13710
13720

Hitchins, 969

Boxall, 15346

15352

Hitchins,
1027
15353

15355

for the ship to change her course to this extent after the helm had been put hard-a-starboard. In this time the ship would travel about 466 yards, and allowing for the few seconds that would be necessary for the order to be given, it may be assumed that 500 yards was about the distance at which the iceberg was sighted either from the bridge or crow's-nest.

That it was quite possible on this night, even with a sharp look-out at the stemhead, crow's-nest and on the bridge, not to see an iceberg at this distance is shown by the evidence of Captain Rostron, of the " Carpathia." Rostron 25401

The injuries to the ship, which are described in the next section, were of such a kind that she foundered in two hours and forty minutes.

3.—DESCRIPTION OF THE DAMAGE TO THE SHIP AND OF ITS GRADUAL AND FINAL EFFECT, WITH OBSERVATIONS THEREON.

The damage done to the ship was as follows :—

Extent of the damage.

The collision with the iceberg, which took place at 11.40 p.m., caused damage to the bottom of the starboard side of the vessel at about 10 feet above the level of the keel, but there was no damage above this height. There was damage in :—

The fore peak, No. 1 hold, No. 2 hold, No. 3 hold, No. 6 boiler room, No. 5 boiler room.

The damage extended over a length of about 300 ft.

Time in which the damage was done.

As the ship was moving at over 20 knots, she would have passed through 300 ft. in less than 10 seconds, so that the damage was done in about this time.

The flooding in first 10 minutes.

At first it is desirable to consider what happened in the first 10 minutes.

The forepeak was not flooded above the Orlop deck—i.e., the peak tank top, from the hole in the bottom of the peak tank.

In No. 1 hold there was 7 ft. of water.

In No. 2 hold five minutes after the collision water was seen rushing in at the bottom of the firemen's passage on the starboard side, so that the ship's side was damaged abaft of bulkhead B sufficiently to open the side of the firemen's passage, which was 3½ ft. from the outer skin of the ship, thereby flooding both the hold and the passage.

In No. 3 hold the mail room was filled soon after the collision. The floor of the mail room is 24 ft. above the keel.

In No. 6 boiler room, when the collision took place, water at once poured in at about 2 feet above the stokehold plates, on the starboard side, at the after end of the boiler room. Some of the firemen immediately went through the watertight door opening to No. 5 boiler room because the water was flooding the place. The watertight doors in the engine-rooms were shut from the bridge almost immediately after the collision. Ten minutes later it was found that there was water to the height of 8 feet above the double bottom in No. 6 boiler room.

No. 5 boiler room was damaged at the ship's side in the starboard forward bunker at a distance of 2 feet above the stokehold plates, at 2 feet from the watertight bulkhead between Nos. 5 and 6 boiler rooms. Water poured in at that place as it would from an ordinary fire hose. At the time of the collision this bunker had no coal in it. The bunker door was closed when water was seen to be entering the ship.

In No. 4 boiler room there was no indication of any damage at the early stages of the sinking.

Gradual effect of the Damage.

It will thus be seen that all the six compartments forward of No. 4 boiler room were open to the sea by damage which existed at about 10 feet above the keel. At 10 minutes after the collision the water seems to have risen to about 14 feet above the keel in all these compartments except No. 5 boiler room. After the first ten minutes, the water rose steadily in all these six compartments. The fore peak above the peak tank was not filled until an hour after the collision when the vessel's bow was submerged to above C deck. The water then flowed in from the top through the deck scuttle forward of the collision bulkhead. It was by this scuttle that access was obtained to all the decks below C down to the peak tank top on the orlop deck.

Poigndestre,
2821-2
Hendrikson,
4859
4856-66
4870
4894

Barrett,
1868
1874
1856
1905
1899
1904
1937
1926

1917
1921
2103
2255
2091
2343

At 12 o'clock water was coming up in No. 1 hatch. It was getting into the firemen's quarters and driving the firemen out. It was rushing round No. 1 hatch on G deck and coming mostly from the starboard side, so that in 20 minutes the water had risen above G deck in No. 1 hold.

In No. 2 hold about 40 minutes after the collision the water was coming in to the seamen's quarters on E deck through a burst fore and aft wooden bulkhead of a third-class cabin opposite the seamen's wash place. Thus, the water had risen in No. 2 hold to about 3 ft. above E deck in 40 minutes.

In No. 3 hold the mail room was afloat about 20 minutes after the collision. The bottom of the mail room which is on the Orlop deck, is 24 feet above the keel.

The watertight doors on F deck at the fore and after ends of No. 3 compartment were not closed then.

The mail room was filling and water was within 2 ft. of G deck, rising fast, when the order was given to clear the boats.

There was then no water on F deck.

There is a stairway on the port side on G deck which leads down to the first-class baggage room on the Orlop deck immediately below. There was water in this baggage room 25 minutes after the collision. Half an hour after the collision water was up to G deck in the mail room.

Thus the water had risen in this compartment to within 2 ft. of G deck in 20 minutes, and above G deck in 25 to 30 minutes.

No. 6 boiler room was abandoned by the men almost immediately after the collision. Ten minutes later the water had risen to 8 ft. above the top of the double bottom, and probably reached the top of the bulkhead at the after end of the compartment, at the level of E deck, in about one hour after the collision.

In No. 5 boiler room there was no water above the stokehold plates, until a rush of water came through the pass between the boilers from the forward end, and drove the leading stoker out.

It has already been shown in the description of what happened in the first ten minutes, that water was coming into No. 5 boiler room in the forward starboard bunker at 2 ft. above the plates in a stream about the size of a deck hose. The door in this bunker had been dropped probably when water was first discovered, which was a few minutes after the collision. This would cause the water to be retained in the bunker until it rose high enough to burst the door which was weaker than the bunker bulkhead. This happened about an hour after the collision.

No. 4 boiler room.—One hour and 40 minutes after collision water was coming in forward, in No. 4 boiler room, from underneath the floor in the forward part, in small quantities. The men remained in that stokehold till ordered on deck.

Nos. 3, 2 and 1 boiler rooms.—When the men left No. 4 some of them went through Nos. 3, 2 and 1 boiler rooms into the reciprocating engine room, and from there on deck. There was no water in the boiler rooms abaft No. 4 one hour 40 minutes after the collision (1.20 a.m.), and there was then none in the reciprocating and turbine engine rooms.

Electrical engine room and tunnels.—There was no damage to these compartments.

From the foregoing it follows that there was no damage abaft No. 4 boiler room.

All the watertight doors aft of the main engine room were opened after the collision.

Half an hour after the collision the watertight doors from the engine room to the stokehold were opened as far forward as they could be to No. 4 boiler room.

Final effect of the Damage.

The later stages of the sinking cannot be stated with any precision, owing to a confusion of the times which was natural under the circumstances.

The forecastle deck was not under water at 1.35 a.m. Distress signals were fired until two hours after the collision (1.45 a.m.). At this time the fore deck was under water. The forecastle head was not then submerged though it was getting close down to the water, about half an hour before she disappeared (1.50 a.m.).

When the last boat, lowered from davits (D), left the ship, A deck was under water, and water came up the stairway under the Boat deck almost immediately

Lee, 2455
2479
2485
Pitman,
14962
14965

Poigndestre
2844
2845
2861

Pitman,
14948
14949

Boxall, 15757
15374
15380

Johnson,
3397

Barrett,
1969
2038
2039
2041

Dillon
3795

3811

Scott,
5599

Lee, 2541
Rowe, 17685
17689
Jewell, 167
Lightoller,
14081
14023
14035

C

afterwards.   After this the other port collapsible (B), which had been stowed on the officers' house, was uncovered, the lashings cut adrift, and she was swung round over the edge of the coamings of the deckhouse on to the Boat deck.

14052
14071
14072

Very shortly afterwards the vessel, according to Mr. Lightoller's account, seemed to take a dive, and he just walked into the water.   When he came to the surface all the funnels were above the water.

14078
14075
14084A
14089
Lee, 2558
Pearcey,10454
Lightoller,
14097

Her stern was gradually rising out of the water, and the propellers were clear of the water.   The ship did not break in two : and she did eventually attain the perpendicular, when the second funnel from aft about reached the water.   There were no lights burning then, though they kept alight practically until the last.

Before reaching the perpendicular when at an angle of 50 or 60 degrees, there was a rumbling sound which may be attributed to the boilers leaving their beds and crashing down on to or through the bulkheads.   She became more perpendicular and finally absolutely perpendicular, when she went slowly down.

2558

After sinking as far as the after part of the Boat deck she went down more quickly.   The ship disappeared at 2.20 a.m.

Observations.

Wilding,
20320

I am advised that the "Titanic" as constructed could not have remained afloat long with such damage as she received.   Her bulkheads were spaced to enable her to remain afloat with any two compartments in communication with the sea. She had a sufficient margin of safety with any two of the compartments flooded which were actually damaged.

20286
20293

20364

In fact any three of the four forward compartments could have been flooded by the damage received without sinking the ship to the top of her bulkheads.

Even if the four forward compartments had been flooded the water would not have got into any of the compartments abaft of them though it would have been above the top of some of the forward bulkheads.   But the ship, even with these four compartments flooded would have remained afloat.   But she could not remain afloat with the four forward compartments and the forward boiler room (No. 6) also flooded.

The flooding of these five compartments alone would have sunk the ship sufficiently deeply to have caused the water to rise above the bulkhead at the after end of the forward boiler room (No. 6) and to flow over into the next boiler room (No. 5), and to fill it up until in turn its after bulkhead would be overwhelmed and the water would thereby flow over and fill No. 4 boiler room, and so on in succession to the other boiler rooms till the ship would ultimately fill and sink.

It has been shown that water came into the five forward compartments to a height of about 14 feet above the keel in the first ten minutes.   This was at a rate of inflow with which the ship's pumps could not possibly have coped, so that the damage done to these five compartments alone inevitably sealed the doom of the ship.

The damage done in the boiler rooms Nos. 5 and 4 was too slight to have hastened appreciably the sinking of the ship, for it was given in evidence that no considerable amount of water was in either of these compartments for an hour after the collision.   The rate at which water came into No. 6 boiler room makes it highly probable that the compartment was filled in not more than an hour, after which the flow over the top of the bulkhead between 5 and 6 began and continued till No. 5 was filled.

Barrett,
2255

It was shown that the leak in No. 5 boiler room was only about equal to the flow of a deck hose pipe about 3 inches in diameter.

Cavell,
4265

3811

The leak in No. 4, supposing that there was one, was only enough to admit about 3 feet of water in that compartment in 1 hour 40 minutes.

Hence the leaks in Nos. 4 and 5 boiler rooms did not appreciably hasten the sinking of the vessel.

Barrett,
1961

The evidence is very doubtful as to No. 4 being damaged.   The pumps were being worked in No. 5 soon after the collision.   The 10 inch leather special suction pipe which was carried from aft is more likely to have been carried for use in No. 5 than No. 4 because the doors were ordered to be opened probably soon after the collision when water was known to be coming into No. 5.   There is no evidence that the pumps were being worked in No. 4.

Scott
5602

The only evidence possibly favourable to the view that the pipe was required for No. 4, and not for No. 5, is that Scott, a greaser, says that he saw engineers dragging the suction pipe along 1 hour after the collision.   But even as late as this it may have been wanted for No. 5 only.

The importance of the question of the damage to No. 5 is small because the ship as actually constructed was doomed as soon as the water in No. 6 boiler room and all compartments forward of it entered in the quantities it actually did.   Wilding
20311-4
20320
20355
20371-4

It is only of importance in dealing with the question of what would have happened to the ship had she been more completely sub-divided.

It was stated in evidence that if No. 4 had not been damaged or had only been damaged to an extent within the powers of the pumps to keep under, then, if the bulkheads had been carried to C deck, the ship might have been saved.   Further methods of increased sub-division and their effect upon the fate of the ship are discussed later.

Evidence was given showing that after the watertight doors in the engine and boiler rooms had been all closed, except those forward of No. 4 group of boilers, they were opened again, and there is no evidence to show that they were again closed.   Though it is probable that the engineers who remained below would have closed these doors as the water rose in the compartments, yet it was not necessary for them to do this as each door had an automatic closing arrangement which would have come into operation immediately a small amount of water came through the door.   Dillon,
3738
3745
3766
3769
3770
3783

It is probable, however, that the life of the ship would have been lengthened somewhat if these doors had been left open, for the water would have flowed through them to the after part of the ship, and the rate of flow of the water into the ship would have been for a time reduced as the bow might have been kept up a little by the water which flowed aft.

It is thus seen that the efficiency of the automatic arrangements for the closing of the watertight doors, which was questioned during the enquiry, had no important bearing on the question of hastening the sinking of the ship, except that, in the case of the doors not having been closed by the engineers, it might have retarded the sinking of the ship if they had not acted.   The engineers would not have prevented the doors from closing unless they had been convinced that the ship was doomed. There is no evidence that they did prevent the doors from closing.

The engineers were applying the pumps when Barrett, leading stoker, left No. 5 boiler room, but even if they had succeeded in getting all the pumps in the ship to work they could not have saved the ship or prolonged her life to any appreciable extent.

Effect of suggested additional sub-division upon floatation.

Watertight decks.—It is in evidence that advantage might be obtained from the point of view of greater safety in having a watertight deck.   Archer,
24424

Without entering into the general question of the advantage of watertight decks for all ships, it is desirable to form an opinion in the case of the " Titanic " as to whether making the bulkhead deck watertight would have been an advantage in the circumstances of the accident, or in case of accident to ships of this class.

I am advised that it is found that with all the compartments certainly known to have been flooded, viz., those forward of No. 4 boiler room, the ship would have remained afloat if the bulkhead deck had been a watertight deck.   If, however, No. 4 boiler room had also been flooded the ship would not have remained afloat unless, in addition to making the bulkhead deck watertight, the transverse bulkhead abaft of No. 4 boiler room had been carried up to D deck.

To make the bulkhead deck effectively watertight for this purpose it would have been necessary to carry watertight trunks round all the openings in the bulkhead deck up to C deck.

It has been shown that with the bulkhead abaft No. 5 boiler room carried to C deck the ship would have remained afloat if the compartments certainly known to have been damaged had been flooded.   518

I do not desire to express an opinion upon the question whether it would have conduced to safety in the case of the " Titanic " if a watertight deck had been fitted below the water line, as there may be some objections to such a deck.   There are many considerations involved, and I think that the matter should be dealt with by the Bulkhead Committee for ships in general.   24426

Wilding,
20209-37
20282-98
25297,8

Longitudinal sub-division.—The advantages and disadvantages of longi-tudinal sub-division by means of watertight bunker bulkheads were pointed out in evidence.

While not attempting to deal with this question generally for ships, I am advised that if the "Titanic" had been divided in the longitudinal method, instead of in the transverse method only, she would have been able, if damaged as supposed, to remain afloat, though with a list which could have been corrected by putting water ballast into suitable places.

This subject is one, however, which again involves many considerations, and I think that for ships generally the matter should be referred to the Bulkhead Committee for their consideration and report.

Extending double bottom up the sides.—It was shown in evidence that there would be increased protection in carrying the double bottom higher up the side than was done in the "Titanic," and that some of the boiler rooms would probably not then have been flooded, as water could not have entered the ship except in the double bottom.

20350-1

In the case of the "Titanic" I am advised that this would have been an advantage, but it was pointed out in evidence that there are certain disadvantages which in some ships may outweigh the advantages.

In view of what has already been said about the possible advantages of longitudinal subdivision, it is unnecessary further to discuss the question of carrying up the double bottom in ships generally. This matter should also be dealt with by the Bulkhead Committee.

Watertight doors.—With reference to the question of the watertight doors of the ship, there does not appear to have been any appreciable effect upon the sinking of the ship caused by either shutting or not shutting the doors. There does not appear to have been any difficulty in working the watertight doors. They appear to have been shut in good time after the collision.

But in other cases of damage in ships constructed like the "Titanic," it is probable that the efficiency of the closing arrangement of the watertight doors may exert a vital influence on the safety of the ship. It has been represented that in future consideration should be given to the question "as to how far bulkheads "should be solid bulkheads, and how far there should be watertight doors, and, if "there should be watertight doors, how far they may or may not be automatically "operated." This again is a question on which it is not necessary here to express any general opinion, for there are conflicting considerations which vary in individual cases. The matter, however, should come under the effective supervision of the Board of Trade much more than it seems to come at present, and should be referred to the Bulkhead Committee for their consideration with a view to their suggesting in detail where doors should or should not be allowed, and the type of door which should be adopted in the different parts of ships.

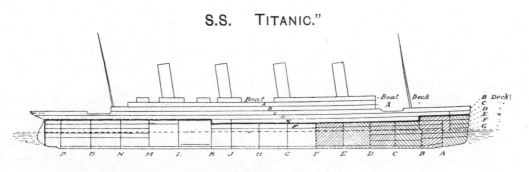

S.S. "TITANIC."

NOTE.—The vertical letters signify the different decks.
 The horizontal letters signify the watertight bulkheads.
 The heavy line shows the top of the watertight bulkheads.
 The crosshatched compartments are those opened to the sea at the time of the collision
  with the iceberg.

4.—ACCOUNT OF THE SAVING AND RESCUE OF THOSE WHO SURVIVED.

The boats.

The " Titanic " was provided with 20 boats. They were all on the Boat deck. Sanderson, 19115–22 Fourteen were life boats. These were hung inboard in davits, seven on the starboard side and seven on the port side, and were designed to carry 65 persons each. Two were emergency boats. These were also in davits, but were hung outboard, one on the starboard side and one on the port side, and were designed to carry 40 persons each. The remaining four boats were Engelhardt or collapsible boats. Two of these were stowed on the Boat deck and two on the roof of the officers' quarters, and were designed to carry 47 persons each. Thus the total boat accommodation was for 1,178 persons. The boats in davits were numbered, the odd numbers being on the starboard side and the even numbers on the port side. The numbering began with the emergency boats which were forward, and ran aft. Thus the boats on the starboard side were numbered 1 (an emergency boat) 3, 5, 7, 9, 11, 13 and 15 (life boats), and those on the port side 2 (an emergency boat), 4, 6, 8, 10, 12, 14 and 16 (life boats). The collapsible boats were lettered, A and B being on the roof of the officers' quarters, and C and D being on the Boat deck; C was abreast of No. 1 (emergency boat) and D abreast of No. 2 (emergency boat). Further particulars as to the boats will be found on page 18.

In ordinary circumstances all these boats (with the exception of 1 and 2) were kept covered up, and contained only a portion of their equipment, such as oars, masts and sails, and water; some of the remaining portion, such as lamps, compasses and biscuits being stowed in the ship in some convenient place, ready for use when required. Much examination was directed at the hearing to showing that some boats left the ship without a lamp and others without a compass and so on, but in the circumstances of confusion and excitement which existed at the time of the disaster this seems to me to be excusable.

Each member of the crew had a boat assigned to him in printed lists which were posted up in convenient places for the men to see; but it appeared that in some cases the men had not looked at these lists and did not know their respective boats.

There had been no proper boat drill nor a boat muster. It was explained that great difficulty frequently exists in getting firemen to take part in a boat drill. They regard it as no part of their work. There seem to be no statutory requirements as to boat drills or musters, although there is a provision (Section 9 of the Merchant Shipping Act of 1906) that when a boat drill does take place the master of the vessel is, under a penalty, to record the fact in his log. I think it is desirable that the Board of Trade should make rules requiring boat drills and boat musters to be held of such a kind and at such times as may be suitable to the ship and to the voyage on which she is engaged. Boat drill, regulated according to the opportunities of the service, should always be held.

It is perhaps worth recording that there was an inspection of the boats Clarke, 24096–103 themselves at Southampton by Mr. Clarke, the emigration officer; and that, as a result, Mr. Clarke gave his certificate that the boats were satisfactory. For the purpose of this inspection two of the boats were lowered to the water and crews exercised in them.

The collision took place at 11.40 p.m. (ship's time). About midnight it was Pitman, 14945 realised that the vessel could not live, and at about 12.5 the order was given to Boxall, 15367 uncover the 14 boats under davits. The work began on both sides of the ship under Lightoller, 13800 the superintendence of five officers. It did not proceed quickly at first; the crew arrived on the Boat deck only gradually, and there was an average of not more than 13819 three deck hands to each boat. At 12.20 the order was given to swing out the boats, Pitman,14992 and this work was at once commenced. There were a few passengers on the deck Lightoller, 13809 at this time. Mr. Lightoller, who was one of the officers directing operations, says Lowe, 15807 that the noise of the steam blowing off was so great that his voice could not be heard, Lightoller, 13811 and that he had to give directions with his hands. Hart, 9926

Before this work had been begun, the stewards were rousing the passengers 9879
Wheat, 10943 in their different quarters, helping them to put on lifebelts and getting them up to 13229 the Boat deck. At about 12.30 the order was given to place women and children in Robinson, 13285

Various
witnesses
15809
14987
14048
10393
13326, 703
13187
13835, 13931,
14011
13929, 13984
13819, 15832
2969, 15832
383
16526, 17926
the boats. This was proceeded with at once and at about 12.45 Mr. Murdoch gave the order to lower No. 7 boat (on the starboard side) to the water. The work of uncovering, filling and lowering the boats was done under the following supervision : Mr. Lowe, the fifth officer, saw to Nos. 1, 3, 5 and 7; Mr. Murdoch (lost) saw also to 1 and 7 and to A and C. Mr. Moody (lost) looked after Nos. 9, 11, 13 and 15. Mr. Murdoch also saw to 9 and 11. Mr. Lightoller saw to Nos. 4, 6, 8, B and D. Mr. Wilde (lost) also saw to 8 and D. Mr. Lightoller and Mr. Moody saw to 10 and 16 and Mr. Lowe to 12 and 14. Mr. Wilde also assisted at No. 14, Mr. Boxall helping generally.

The evidence satisfies me that the officers did their work very well and without any thought of themselves. Captain Smith, the Master, Mr. Wilde, the chief officer, Mr Murdoch, the first officer, and Mr. Moody, the sixth officer, all went down with the ship while performing their duties. The others, with the exception of Mr. Lightoller, took charge of boats and thus were saved. Mr. Lightoller was swept off the deck as the vessel went down and was subsequently picked up.

15809, 147,
156, 15593,
15000, 17911,
4937, 4987,
11071, 2134,
10120, 13303,
13200, 2266,
5647, 10456,
5950, 1018,
1054, 1085,
1094, 13931,
5841, 17920,
14014, 15426,
15832, 14068
So far as can be ascertained the boats left the ship at the following times, but I think it is necessary to say that these, and, indeed, all the times subsequent to the collision which are mentioned by the witnesses, are unreliable :—

No.	Starboard side.	No.	Port side.
7	At 12.45 a.m.	6	At 12.55 a.m.
5	„ 12.55	8	„ 1.10
3	„ 1.0	10	„ 1.20
1	„ 1.10	12	„ 1.25
9	„ 1.20	14	„ 1.30
11	„ 1.25	16	„ 1.35
13	„ 1.35	2	„ 1.45
15	„ 1.35	4	„ 1.55
C	„ 1.40	D	„ 2.5
A	Floated off when the ship sank and was utilised as a raft.	B	Floated off when the ship sank and was utilised as a raft.

Brown, 10530
Lightoller,
14011
14035
As regards the collapsible boats, C and D were properly lowered; as to A and B, which were on the roof of the officers' house, they were left until the last. There was difficulty in getting these boats down to the deck, and the ship had at this time a list. Very few of the deck hands were left in the ship, as they had nearly all gone to man the lifeboats, and the stewards and firemen were unaccustomed to work the collapsible boats. Work appears to have been going on in connection with these two boats at the time that the ship sank. The boats seem to have floated Brown, 10542
Lightoller,
14069 from the deck and to have served in the water as rafts.

The following table shows the numbers of the male crew, male passengers, and women and children who, according to the evidence, left the ship in each boat. In three or four instances the numbers of women and children are only arrived at by subtracting the numbers of crew and male passengers from the total said to be in the boat (these are in italics). In each case the lowest figures given are taken :—

Starboard Side Boat. No.	Men of Crew.	Men Passengers.	Women and Children.	Total.	Port Side Boat. No.	Men of Crew.	Men Passengers.	Women and Children.	Total.
7	3	4	*20*	27	6	2	2	*24*	28
5	5	6	30	41	8	4	—	35	39
3	15	10	*25*	50	10	5	—	50	55
1	7	3	2	12	2	4	1	21	26
9	8	6	42	56	12	2	—	40	42
11	9	1	60	70	14	8		53	63
13	5	—	59	64	16	6	—	50	56
15	13	4	*53*	70	4	4	—	36	40
C	5	2	64	71	D	2	2	40	44
A utilized after the ship sank.					B utilized after the ship sank.				
Totals	70	36	*355*	461		37	7	349	393

General Total   ...   107 men of the crew.
43 men passengers.
704 women and children.

This shows in all 107 men of the crew, 43 male passengers and 704 women and children, or a total of 854 in 18 boats. In addition, about 60 persons, two of whom were women, were said to have been transferred, subsequently, from A and B collapsible boats to other boats, or rescued from the water, making a total of 914 who escaped with their lives. It is obvious that these figures are quite unreliable, for only 712 were, in fact, saved by the "Carpathia," the steamer which came to the rescue at about 4 a.m., and all the boats were accounted for. Another remarkable discrepancy is that, of the 712 saved, 189 were, in fact, men of the crew, 129 were male passengers and 394 were women and children. In other words, the real proportion of women to men saved was much less than the proportion appearing in the evidence from the boats. Allowing for those subsequently picked up, of the 712 persons saved only 652 can have left the "Titanic" in boats, or an average of about 36 per boat. There was a tendency in the evidence to exaggerate the numbers in each boat, to exaggerate the proportion of women to men and to diminish the number of crew. I do not attribute this to any wish on the part of the witnesses to mislead the Court, but to a natural desire to make the best case for themselves and their ship. The seamen who gave evidence were too frequently encouraged when under examination in the witness-box to understate the number of crew in the boats. The number of crew actually saved was 189, giving an average of ten per boat : and if from this figure the 58 men of the 60 persons above mentioned be deducted the average number of crew leaving the ship in the boats must still have been at least 7. The probability, however, is that many of the 60 picked up were passengers.

The discipline both among passengers and crew during the lowering of the boats was good, but the organisation should have been better, and if it had been it is possible that more lives would have been saved. [Various Witnesses, 104, 723, 14006, 1504, 6448]

The real difficulty in dealing with the question of the boats is to find the explanation of so many of them leaving the ship with comparatively few persons in them. No. 1 certainly left with only 12; this was an emergency boat with a carrying capacity of 40. No. 7 left with only 27, and No. 6 with only 28; these were lifeboats with a carrying capacity of 65 each; and several of the others, according to the evidence and certainly according to the truth, must have left only partly filled. Many explanations are forthcoming, one being that the passengers were unwilling to leave the ship. When the earlier boats left, and before the "Titanic" had begun materially to settle down, there was a drop of 65 feet from the Boat deck to the water, and the women feared to get into the boats. Many people thought that the risk in the ship was less than the risk in the boats. This explanation is supported by the evidence of Captain Rostron of the "Carpathia." He says that after those who were saved got on board his ship, he was told by some of them that when the boats first left the "Titanic" the people "really would not be put "in the boats; they did not want to go in." There was a large body of evidence from the "Titanic" to the same effect, and I have no doubt that many people, particularly women, refused to leave the deck for the boats. At one time the Master appears to have had the intention of putting the people into the boats from the gangway doors in the side of the ship. This was possibly with a view to allay the fears of the passengers, for from these doors the water could be reached by means of ladders, and the lowering of some of the earlier boats when only partly filled may be accounted for in this way. There is no doubt that the Master did order some of the partly filled boats to row to a position under one of the doors with the object of taking in passengers at that point. It appears, however, that these doors were never opened. Another explanation is that some women refused to leave their husbands. It is said further that the officers engaged in putting the people into the boats feared that the boats might buckle if they were filled; but this proved to be an unfounded apprehension, for one or more boats were completely filled and then successfully lowered to the water. [1127, 1146, 5955, 13996, 15931, 9924, 25566] [131, 13896, 15906, 14186, 15451] [13887, 13954, 16011, 17897, 2156]

At 12.35 the message from the "Carpathia" was received announcing that she was making for the "Titanic." This probably became known and may have tended to make the passengers still more unwilling to leave the ship : and the lights of a ship (the "Californian") which were seen by many people may have encouraged the passengers to hope that assistance was at hand. These explanations are perhaps sufficient to account for so many of the lifeboats leaving without a full boat load; but I think, nevertheless, that if the boats had been kept a little longer before being lowered, or if the after gangway doors had been opened, more passengers might have been induced to enter the boats. And if women could [Bride, 16798] not be induced to enter the boats, the boats ought then to have been filled up with men. It is difficult to account for so many of the lifeboats being sent from the sinking ship, in a smooth sea, far from full. These boats left behind them many hundreds of lives to perish. I do not, however, desire these observations to be read as casting any reflection on the officers of the ship or on the crew who were working on the Boat deck. They all worked admirably, but I think that if there had been better organisation the results would have been more satisfactory.

I heard much evidence as to the conduct of the boats after the "Titanic" sank and when there must have been many struggling people in the water, and I regret to say that in my opinion some, at all events, of the boats failed to attempt to save lives when they might have done so, and might have done so successfully. This was particularly the case with boat No. 1. It may reasonably have been thought that the risk of making the attempt was too great; but it seems to me that if the attempt had been made by some of these boats it might have been the means of saving a few more lives. Subject to these few adverse comments, I have nothing but praise for both passengers and crew. All the witnesses speak well of their behaviour. It is to be remembered that the night was dark, the noise of the escaping steam was terrifying, the peril, though perhaps not generally recognised, was imminent and great, and many passengers who were unable to speak or to understand English, were being collected together and hurried into the boats.

Hendrikson, 5011
Symons, 11501 11527

Conduct of Sir C. Duff Gordon and Mr. Ismay.

An attack was made in the course of the Enquiry on the moral conduct of two of the passengers, namely, Sir Cosmo Duff Gordon and Mr. Bruce Ismay. It is no part of the business of the Court to enquire into such matters, and I should pass them by in silence if I did not fear that my silence might be misunderstood. The very gross charge against Sir Cosmo Duff Gordon that, having got into No. 1 boat he bribed the men in it to row away from drowning people is unfounded. I have said that the members of the crew in that boat might have made some attempt to save the people in the water, and that such an attempt would probably have been successful; but I do not believe that the men were deterred from making the attempt by any act of Sir Cosmo Duff Gordon's. At the same time I think that if he had encouraged the men to return to the position where the "Titanic" had foundered they would probably have made an effort to do so and could have saved some lives.

Duff Gordon, 12586 et seq.

As to the attack on Mr. Bruce Ismay, it resolved itself into the suggestion that, occupying the position of Managing Director of the Steamship Company, some moral duty was imposed upon him to wait on board until the vessel foundered. I do not agree. Mr. Ismay, after rendering assistance to many passengers, found "C" collapsible, the last boat on the starboard side, actually being lowered. No other people were there at the time. There was room for him and he jumped in. Had he not jumped in he would merely have added one more life, namely, his own, to the number of those lost.

Ismay, 18559

The third-class passengers.

It had been suggested before the Enquiry that the third-class passengers had been unfairly treated; that their access to the Boat deck had been impeded, and that when at last they reached that deck the first and second-class passengers were given precedence in getting places in the boats. There appears to have been no truth in these suggestions. It is no doubt true that the proportion of third-class passengers saved falls far short of the proportion of the first and second class, but this is accounted for by the greater reluctance of the third-class passengers to leave the ship, by their unwillingness to part with their baggage, by the difficulty in getting them up from their quarters, which were at the extreme ends of the ship, and by other similar causes. The interests of the relatives of some of the third-class passengers who had perished were in the hands of Mr. Harbinson, who attended the Enquiry on their behalf. He said at the end of his address to the Court : "I wish to say dis- "tinctly that no evidence has been given in the course of this case which would "substantiate a charge that any attempt was made to keep back the third-class "passengers. . . . I desire further to say that there is no evidence that when "they did reach the boat deck there was any discrimination practised either by the "officers or the sailors in putting them into the boats."

I am satisfied that the explanation of the excessive proportion of third-class passengers lost is not to be found in the suggestion that the third-class passengers were in any way unfairly treated.   They were not unfairly treated.

Means taken to procure assistance.

As soon as the dangerous condition of the ship was realised, messages were sent by the Master's orders to all steamers within reach.   At **12.15 a.m.** the distress signal C.Q.D. was sent.   This was heard by several steamships and by Cape Race.   By **12.25**, Mr. Boxall, the fourth officer, had worked out the correct position of the "Titanic," and then another message was sent: "Come at once, we have struck a berg."   This was heard by the Cunard steamer "Carpathia," which was at this time bound from New York to Liverpool and 58 miles away.   The "Carpathia" answered, saying that she was coming to the assistance of the "Titanic." This was reported to Captain Smith on the Boat deck.   At **12.26** a message was sent out, "Sinking; cannot hear for noise of steam."   Many other messages were also sent, but as they were only heard by steamers which were too far away to render help it is not necessary to refer to them.   At **1.45** a message was heard by the "Carpathia," "Engine room full up to boilers."   The last message sent out was "C.Q.," which was faintly heard by the steamer "Virginian."   This message was sent at **2.17**.   It thus appears that the Marconi apparatus was at work until within a few minutes of the foundering of the "Titanic."

Meanwhile Mr. Boxall was sending up distress signals from the deck.   These signals (rockets) were sent off at intervals from a socket by No. 1 emergency boat on the Boat deck.   They were the ordinary distress signals, exploding in the air and throwing off white stars.   The firing of these signals began about the time that No. 7 boat was lowered (**12.45 a.m.**), and it continued until Mr. Boxall left the ship at about **1.45**.

Mr. Boxall was also using a Morse light from the bridge in the direction of a ship whose lights he saw about half a point on the port bow of the "Titanic" at a distance, as he thought, of about five or six miles.   He got no answer.   In all, Mr. Boxall fired about eight rockets.   There appears to be no doubt that the vessel whose lights he saw was the "Californian." The evidence from the "Californian" speaks of eight rockets having been seen between **12.30** and **1.40**.   The "Californian" heard none of the "Titanic's" messages; she had only one Marconi operator on board and he was asleep.

The rescue by the S.S. "Carpathia."

On the 15th of April the s.s. "Carpathia," 13,600 tons gross, of the Cunard Line, Mr. Arthur Henry Rostron, Master, was on her passage to Liverpool from New York.   She carried some 740 passengers and 325 crew.

On receipt of the "Titanic's" first distress message the Captain immediately ordered the ship to be turned round and driven at her highest speed (17½ knots) in the direction of the "Titanic."   He also informed the "Titanic" by wireless that he was coming to her assistance, and he subsequently received various messages from her.   At about 2.40 a.m. he saw a green flare which, as the evidence shows, was being sent up by Mr. Boxall in No. 2 boat.   From this time until 4 a.m. Captain Rostron was altering his course continually in order to avoid icebergs.   He fired rockets in answer to the signals he saw from Boxall's boat.   At 4 o'clock he considered he was practically up to the position given and he stopped his ship at 4.5.   He sighted the first boat (No. 2) and picked her up at 4.10.   There was then a large number of icebergs round him, and it was just daylight.   Eventually he picked up in all 13 lifeboats, two emergency boats and two collapsible boats, all of which were taken on board the "Carpathia," the other boats being abandoned as damaged or useless.   From these boats he took on board 712 persons, one of whom died shortly afterwards.   The boats were scattered over an area of four to five miles, and it was 8 a.m. before they had all been picked up.   He saw very little wreckage when he got near to the scene of the disaster, only a few deck chairs, cork lifebelts, etc., and only one body.   The position was then 41° 46′ N., 50° 14′ W.

The "Carpathia" subsequently returned to New York with the passengers and crew she had rescued.

The Court desires to record its great admiration of Captain Rostron's conduct.   He did the very best that could be done.

(Marginal references:)
Bride, 16508
Boxall, 15390
Bride, 16517
Cottam, 17114
Boxall, 15394
15593
15420
Lightoller. 14160
Gill, 18156-61
Stone 7830 et seq.
Rostron, 25361 et seq.
25385
25390
25401
25551

Numbers saved.

The following were the numbers saved :—

1st class.

Adult males	57	out of 175 or 32·57 per cent.
Adult females	140	out of 144 or 97.22 ,,
Male children	5	All saved.
Female children	1	All saved.
	203	out of 325 or 62.46 ,,

2nd class.

Adult males	14	out of 168 or 8.33 per cent.
Adult females	80	out of 93 or 86.02 ,,
Male children	11	All saved.
Female children	13	All saved.
	118	out of 285 or 41.40 ,,

3rd class.

Adult males	75	out of 462 or 16.23 per cent.
Adult females	76	out of 165 or 46.06 ,,
Male children	13	out of 48 or 27.08 ,,
Female children	14	out of 31 or 45.16 ,,
	178	out of 706 or 25.21 ,,
Total	499	out of 1,316 or 37.94 ,,

Crew saved.

Deck Department ...	43	out of 66 or 65.15 per cent.
Engine. Room Department	72	out of 325 or 22.15 ,,
Victualling Department, (including 20 women out of 23)	97	out of 494 or 19.63 ,,
Total...	212	out of 885 or 23.95 ,,
Total on board saved .	711	out of 2,201 or 32.30 ,,

Passengers and Crew.

Adult males	338	out of 1,667 or 20·27 per cent.
Adult females	316	out of 425 or 74·35 ,,
Children	57	out of 109 or 52·29 ,,
Total	711	out of 2,201 or 32·30 ,,

5.—THE CIRCUMSTANCES IN CONNECTION WITH THE S.S. "CALIFORNIAN."

It is here necessary to consider the circumstances relating to the s.s. "Californian."

On the 14th of April, the s.s. "Californian" of the Leyland Line, Mr. Stanley Lord, Master, was on her passage from London, which port she left on April 5th, to Boston, U.S., where she subsequently arrived on April 19th. She was a vessel of 6,223 tons gross and 4,038 net. Her full speed was 12½ to 13 knots. She had a passenger certificate, but was not carrying any passengers at the time. She belonged to the International Mercantile Marine Company, the owners of the "Titanic."

At 7.30 p.m., ship's time, on 14th April, a wireless message was sent from this ship to the "Antillian." "To Captain, 'Antillian,' 6.30 p.m., apparent ship's "time, lat. 42° 3′ N., long. 49° 9′ W. Three large bergs, 5 miles to southward of us. "Regards.—Lord." Evans, 8941, 8943

The message was intercepted by the "Titanic," and when the Marconi operator (Evans) of the "Californian" offered this ice report to the Marconi operator of the "Titanic," shortly after 7.30 p.m., the latter replied, "It is all "right. I heard you sending it to the 'Antillian,' and I have got it." 8972
Lord, 6710

The "Californian" proceeded on her course S. 89° W. true until 10.20 p.m., ships' time, when she was obliged to stop and reverse engines because she was running into field ice, which stretched as far as could then be seen to the northward and southward.

The Master told the Court that he made her position at that time to be 42° 5′ N., 57° 7′ W. This position is recorded in the log book, which was written up from the scrap log book by the Chief Officer. The scrap log is destroyed. It is a position about 19 miles N. by E. of the position of the "Titanic" when she foundered, and is said to have been fixed by dead reckoning and verified by observations. I am satisfied that this position is not accurate. The Master "twisted her "head" to E.N.E. by the compass and she remained approximately stationary until 5.15 a.m. on the following morning. The ship was slowly swinging round to starboard during the night. 6704

Lord, 6713
Groves, 8249

At about 11 p.m. a steamer's light was seen approaching from the eastward. The Master went to Evans' room and asked, "What ships he had." The latter replied: "I think the 'Titanic' is near us. I have got her." The Master said: "You had better advise the 'Titanic' we are stopped and surrounded with ice." This Evans did, calling up the "Titanic" and sending: "We are stopped and surrounded by ice." The "Titanic" replied: "Keep out." The "Titanic" was in communication with Cape Race, which station was then sending messages to her. The reason why the "Titanic" answered, "Keep out," was that her Marconi operator could not hear what Cape Race was saying, as from her proximity, the message from the "Californian" was much stronger than any message being taken in by the "Titanic" from Cape Race, which was much further off. Evans heard the "Titanic" continuing to communicate with Cape Race up to the time he turned in at 11.30 p.m. Evans, 8982
8988

8993
8994
9004

9022

The Master of the "Californian" states that when observing the approaching steamer as she got nearer, he saw more lights, a few deck lights, and also her green side light. He considered that at 11 o'clock she was approximately six or seven miles away, and at some time between 11 and 11.30, he first saw her green light, she was then about 5 miles off. He noticed that about 11.30 she stopped. In his opinion this steamer was of about the same size as the "Californian"; a medium-sized steamer, "something like ourselves." Lord, 6761

6752

From the evidence of Mr. Groves, third officer of the "Californian," who was the officer of the first watch, it would appear that the Master was not actually on the bridge when the steamer was sighted.

Mr. Groves made out two masthead lights; the steamer was changing her bearing slowly as she got closer, and as she approached he went to the chart room and reported this to the Master; he added, "she is evidently a passenger steamer." In fact, Mr. Groves never appears to have had any doubt on this subject; in answer to a question during his examination, "Had she much light," he said, "Yes, a lot Groves, 8147

8174

8178

"of light. There was absolutely no doubt of her being a passenger steamer, at
"least in my mind."

Gill, 18136   Gill, the assistant donkey-man of the "Californian," who was on deck at
midnight said, referring to this steamer: "It could not have been anything but a
"passenger boat, she was too large."

Groves, 8182   By the evidence of Mr. Groves, the Master, in reply to his report, said:
"Call her up on the Morse lamp, and see if you can get any answer." This he proceeded to do. The Master came up and joined him on the bridge and remarked:
8197   "That does not look like a passenger steamer." Mr. Groves replied "It is, Sir.
"When she stopped, her lights seemed to go out, and I suppose they have been put
8203   "out for the night." Mr. Groves states that these lights went out at 11.40, and
8217   remembers that time because "one bell was struck to call the middle watch." The
Master did not join him on the bridge until shortly afterwards, and consequently
after the steamer had stopped.

In his examination Mr. Groves admitted that if this steamer's head was
turning to port after she stopped, it might account for the diminution of lights,
8228   by many of them being shut out. Her steaming lights were still visible and also her
port side light.

8241   The Captain only remained upon the bridge for a few minutes. In his evi-
Lord, 6866   dence he stated that Mr. Groves had made no observations to him about the steamer's
deck lights going out. Mr. Groves' Morse signalling appears to have been
ineffectual (although at one moment he thought he was being answered), and he
Groves,   gave it up. He remained on the bridge until relieved by Mr. Stone, the second officer,
8244-51   just after midnight. In turning the "Californian" over to him, he pointed out
the steamer and said: "she has been stopped since 11.40; she is a passenger steamer.
Stone, 7810   "At about the moment she stopped she put her lights out." When Mr. Groves
Groves, 8441   was in the witness-box the following questions were put to him by me: "Speaking
"as an experienced seaman and knowing what you do know now, do you think that
"steamer that you know was throwing up rockets, and that you say was a passen-
"ger steamer, was the 'Titanic'?—Do I think it? Yes?—From what I have heard
"subsequently? Yes?—Most decidedly I do, but I do not put myself as being
"an experienced man. But that is your opinion as far as your experience goes?—
"Yes, it is, my Lord."

Stone, 7815   Mr. Stone states that the Master, who was also up (but apparently not on the
bridge), pointed out the steamer to him with instructions to tell him if her bearings
altered or if she got any closer; he also stated that Mr. Groves had called her up
on the Morse lamp and had received no reply.

Mr. Stone had with him during the middle watch an apprentice named
Gibson, 7424   Gibson, whose attention was first drawn to the steamer's lights at about 12.20 a.m.
He could see a masthead light, her red light (with glasses) and a "glare of white
"lights on her after deck." He first thought her masthead light was flickering
7443   and next thought it was a Morse light, "calling us up." He replied, but could
Gill, 18156-61   not get into communication, and finally came to the conclusion that it was, as he
had first supposed, the masthead light flickering. Some time after 12.30 a.m.,
Gill, the donkeyman, states that he saw two rockets fired from the ship which he
had been observing, and about 1.10 a.m., Mr. Stone reported to the Captain by voice
Stone, 7870   pipe, that he had seen five white rockets from the direction of the steamer. He
states that the Master answered, "Are they Company's signals?" and that he
replied, "I do not know, but they appear to me to be white rockets." The Master
told him to "go on Morsing," and, when he received any information, to send the
7879   apprentice down to him with it. Gibson states that Mr. Stone informed him that
he had reported to the Master, and that the Master had said the steamer was to be
Gibson, 7479   called up by Morse light. This witness thinks the time was 12.55; he at once
proceeded again to call the steamer up by Morse. He got no reply, but the vessel
fired three more white rockets; these rockets were also seen by Mr. Stone.

Both Mr. Stone and the apprentice kept the steamer under observation,
looking at her from time to time with their glasses. Between 1 o'clock and 1.40
some conversation passed between them. Mr. Stone remarked to Gibson: "Look at
7515   "her now, she looks very queer out of water, her lights look queer." He also is
7529   said by Gibson to have remarked, "A ship is not going to fire rockets at sea for
Stone, 7894   "nothing;" and admits himself that he may possibly have used that expression.

Mr. Stone states that he saw the last of the rockets fired at about 1.40, and
after watching the steamer for some twenty minutes more he sent Gibson down to
7949   the Master. "I told Gibson to go down to the Master, and be sure and wake him, and

"tell him that altogether we had seen eight of these white lights like white rockets in "the direction of this other steamer; that this steamer was disappearing in the "south-west, that we had called her up repeatedly on the Morse lamp and received "no information whatsoever."

Gibson states that he went down to the chart room and told the Master; that the Master asked him if all the rockets were white, and also asked him the time. Gibson stated that at this time the Master was awake. It was five minutes past two, and Gibson returned to the bridge to Mr. Stone and reported. They both continued to keep the ship under observation until she disappeared. Mr. Stone describes this as "A gradual disappearing of all her lights, which would be perfectly "natural with a ship steaming away from us." *Gibson, 7553* *Stone, 7957*

At about 2.40 a.m. Mr. Stone again called up the Master by voice pipe and told him that the ship from which he had seen the rockets come had disappeared bearing S.W. ½ W., the last he had seen of the light; and the Master again asked him if he was certain there was no colour in the lights. "I again assured him they were all white, just white rockets." There is considerable discrepancy between the evidence of Mr. Stone and that of the Master. The latter states that he went to the voice pipe at about 1.15, but was told then of a white rocket (not five white rockets). Moreover, between 1.30 and 4.30, when he was called by the chief officer (Mr. Stewart), he had no recollection of anything being reported to him at all, although he remembered Gibson opening and closing the chart room door. *7976* *7999* *Lord, 6790* *6859*

Mr. Stewart relieved Mr. Stone at 4 a.m. The latter told him he had seen a ship four or five miles off when he went on deck at 12 o'clock, and at 1 o'clock he had seen some white rockets, and that the moment the ship started firing them she started to steam away. Just at this time (about 4 a.m.) a steamer came in sight with two white masthead lights and a few lights amidships. He asked Mr. Stone whether he thought this was the steamer which had fired rockets, and Mr. Stone said he did not think it was. At 4.30 he called the Master and informed him that Mr. Stone had told him he had seen rockets in the middle watch. The Master said, "Yes, I know, he has been telling me." The Master came at once on to the bridge, and apparently took the fresh steamer for the one which had fired rockets, and said, "She looks all right; she is not making any signals now." This mistake was not corrected. He, however, had the wireless operator called. *Stewart, 8577* *8582* *8598* *8615* *8619* *8632*

At about 6 a.m. Captain Lord heard from the "Virginian" that 'the "'Titanic' had struck a berg, passengers in boats, ship sinking"; and he at once started through the field ice at full speed for the position given. *Lord, 7002*

Captain Lord stated that about 7.30 a.m. he passed the "Mount Temple" stopped, and that she was in the vicinity of the position given him as where the "Titanic" had collided (lat. 41° 46′ N.; long. 50° 14′ W.). He saw no wreckage there, but did later on near the "Carpathia," which ship he closed soon afterwards. and he stated that the position where he subsequently left this wreckage was 41° 33′ N.; 50° 1′ W. It is said in the evidence of Mr. Stewart that the position of the "Californian" was verified by stellar observations at 7.30 p.m. on the Sunday evening, and that he verified the Captain's position given when the ship stopped (42° 5′ N.; 50° 7′ W.) as accurate on the next day. The position in which the wreckage was said to have been seen on the Monday morning was verified by sights taken on that morning. *7014* *7026* *7030*

All the officers are stated to have taken sights, and Mr. Stewart in his evidence remarks that they all agreed. If it is admitted that these positions were correct, then it follows that the "Titanic's" position as given by that ship when making the C.Q.D. signal was approximately S. 16° W. (true), 19 miles from the "Californian"; and further that the position in which the "Californian" was stopped during the night, was thirty miles away from where the wreckage was seen by her in the morning, or that the wreckage had drifted eleven miles in a little more than five hours. *Stewart, 8820*

There are contradictions and inconsistencies in the story as told by the different witnesses. But the truth of the matter is plain. The "Titanic" collided with the berg at 11.40. The vessel seen by the "Californian" stopped at this time. The rockets sent up from the "Titanic" were distress signals. The "Californian" saw distress signals. The number sent up by the "Titanic" was about eight. The "Californian" saw eight. The time over which the rockets from the "Titanic" were sent up was from about 12.45 to 1.45 o'clock. It was about this time that the "Californian" saw the rockets. At 2.40 Mr. Stone called to the Master that the ship from which he had seen the rockets had disappeared. *7020*

At 2.20 a.m. the "Titanic" had foundered.   It was suggested that the rockets seen by the "Californian" were from some other ship, not the "Titanic." But no other ship to fit this theory has ever been heard of.

These circumstances convince me that the ship seen by the "Californian" was the "Titanic," and if so, according to Captain Lord, the two vessels were about five miles apart at the time of the disaster.   The evidence from the "Titanic" corroborates this estimate, but I am advised that the distance was probably greater, though not more than eight to ten miles.   The ice by which the "Californian" was surrounded was loose ice extending for a distance of not more than two or three miles in the direction of the "Titanic."   The night was clear and the sea was smooth.   When she first saw the rockets the "Californian" could have pushed through the ice to the open water without any serious risk and so have come to the assistance of the "Titanic."   Had she done so she might have saved many if not all of the lives that were lost.

6.—THE BOARD OF TRADE'S ADMINISTRATION.

The Court was invited by the Board of Trade "to report upon the Rules and B. T. Deptl.
"Regulations made under the Merchant Shipping Acts 1894-1906, and the Pap. 246.
"administration of those Acts, and of such Rules and Regulations so far as the
"consideration thereof is material to this casualty" (No. 26 of the Questions submitted to the Court by the Board of Trade). Charges were made against the Board
of Trade during the progress of the Enquiry of a twofold kind. First it was said
that the Board had been negligent in that they had failed to keep up to date their
Rules and Regulations relating generally to the provision of life saving appliances
at sea, and secondly it was said that their officials had in the particular instance
of the "Titanic" failed to exercise due care in the supervision of the vessel's plans
and the inspection of the work done upon her.

With reference to the first of these charges, it was reduced in the course of Howell, 22263
the Enquiry to a charge of neglect to keep the Board's scale for the provision of
lifeboat accommodation up to date. The circumstances are these. In March,
1886, the Board appointed a Departmental Committee consisting of three of their
principal officers to enquire into the question of boats, rafts and life-saving
apparatus carried by sea-going merchant ships. In their report this Committee
pointed out that as regards boats for ocean-going steamers carrying large numbers
of passengers, the boats would be of little use in saving life (although they might
for a time prolong its existence) unless succour were at hand from other ships, or
from proximity to shore; and speaking with special reference to passenger steam
vessels carrying emigrants across the Atlantic to ports on the east coast of North
America, they said as follows:—

"Considering the number of vessels employed in this trade, and the
"large number of passengers they carry, and also taking into consideration
"the stormy character of the ocean they have to cross, and the thick and
"foggy weather encountered, we think this class is the most important of
"any, and we cannot pass over the fact that of late years this traffic has
"been carried on with remarkable immunity from loss of life.

"The boat accommodation these vessels are forced to carry when
"sailing with emigrants is regulated by the scale in the Passengers Act,
"1855, which provides for boat accommodation for 216 people as a maxi-
"mum, so that supposing a vessel leaves with 1,000 passengers and 200
"crew under the present statutory requirements, she need only carry
"sufficient boat accommodation for 216 of these people. Thus it will be
"seen that the boats carried by this class of vessel are also quite inadequate
"as an effectual means of saving life should a disaster happen to a ship
"with her full complement of passengers on board. We are glad to be
"able to say that there are many liberal and careful shipowners who do
"all in their power to provide for the safety of their passengers by equip-
"ping their vessels with boats far in excess of the number required by
"statute. But, at the same time, there are others carrying large numbers
"of emigrants who do no more than they are required to do by law.

"We have gone into this question with reference to this class of vessel
"very fully, and have visited many of them, and we think that the boats
"required by Act should be increased 100 per cent., and in addition to
"them that the owners should be induced to carry sufficient collapsible
"boats and approved rafts, so that each ship shall have sufficient life-
"saving gear for all on board at any one time, provided, as said before,
"that no ship need carry more boat accommodation than is sufficient for
"all on board at that time."

In 1887 a Select Committee of the House of Commons, of which Lord Charles 22272-5
Beresford was the Chairman, was appointed to report on Saving Life at Sea, and
they found in their report "That many passenger ships could not, without great
"inconvenience, carry so many of the ordinary wooden boats as would suffice to
"carry the whole of the passengers and crew with safety in bad weather. Under
"such circumstances the crew would not be sufficient to man so many boats; nor
"could they all be got into the water in sufficient time in the event of very rapid

" foundering. Having regard, however, to the fact that accidents occur probably
" as often in moderate weather as in bad, and having regard also to the fact that
" the very cause of the accident frequently incapacitates many of the boats, and
" to the further fact that an insufficiency of boats undoubtedly tends to cause panic,
" we are of opinion that all sea-going passenger ships should be compelled by law to
" carry such boats, and other life-saving apparatus, as would in the aggregate best
" provide for the safety of all on board in moderate weather."

As a result of these reports, the "Merchant Shipping (Life Saving Appli-
" ances) Act, 1888," appears to have been passed, under which rules were made by
the Board of Trade at different dates. The Merchant Shipping Act, 1894, repealed
the Act of 1888, and substituted therefor sections 427 to 431 and the seventeenth
schedule of the new Act. Under this Act (1894), a Table showing the minimum
number of boats to be placed under davits, and their minimum cubic contents was
issued by the Board. It was dated the 9 March, 1894, and came into operation
on the 1 June of that year. This table was based on the gross tonnage of the vessels
to which it was to apply, and not upon the numbers carried, and it provided that
the number of boats and their capacity should increase as the tonnage increased.
The table, however, stopped short at the point where the gross tonnage of the
vessels reached " 10,000 and upwards." As to all such vessels, whatever their size
might be, the minimum number of boats under davits was fixed by the table at 16,
with a total minimum capacity of 5,500 cubic feet.

But as regarded emigrant steamships there was a rule which provided that
if the boats under davits required by the table did not furnish sufficient accommodation for all on board, then additional boats of approved description (whether under
davits or not) or approved life rafts should be carried, and that these additional
boats or rafts should be of at least such carrying capacity that they and the boats
required by the table should provide together in vessels of 5,000 tons and upwards
three-fourths more than the minimum cubic contents required by the table, so that in
the case of an emigrant ship such as the " Titanic " the requirements under the rules
and table together exacted a provision of 9,625 cubic feet of lifeboat and raft
accommodation (5,500 feet in boats under davits with three-fourths, namely, 4,125,
added). Taken at 10 cubic feet per person, this would be equivalent to a provision
for 962 persons. No doubt at the time these rules were made and this table was
drawn up it was thought that, having regard to the size of vessels then built and
building, it was unnecessary to carry the table further. The largest emigrant
steamer then afloat was the " Lucania," of 12,952 tons.

In the report of the Select Committee of the House of Commons a reference
to watertight bulkheads had been made, which was in the following terms :—

" Though the question of construction was clearly not included in the
reference to the Committee, still they think it only right to state, after
having heard the evidence, that the proper placing of bulkheads, so as to
enable a ship to keep afloat for some length of time after an accident has
occurred, is most important for saving life at sea, and a thing upon which
the full efficiency of life-saving appliances largely depends."

This passage probably explains the insertion in the Board of Trade's
Rules for Life Saving Appliances of Rule No. 12, which is as follows :—

" *Watertight compartments.*—When ships of any class are divided
" into efficient watertight compartments to the satisfaction of the Board
" of Trade, they shall only be required to carry additional boats, rafts
" and buoyant apparatus of one-half of the capacity required by these
" Rules, but the exemption shall not extend to life-jackets or similar
" approved articles of equal buoyancy suitable to be worn on the person."

If this rule had become applicable to the " Titanic," then the total cubical
lifeboat or raft accommodation which she would have been required to carry would
not have been more than 7,562 (equivalent to accommodation for 756 persons). It
did not, however, become applicable for the owners never required the Board of
Trade to express any opinion under the rule as to the efficiency of the watertight
compartments. The " Titanic," in fact, carried boat accommodation for 1,178
persons, a number far in excess of the requirements of the Table and Rules, and
therefore no concession under Rule 12 was needed. Speaking generally, recourse
to this Rule (12) by shipowners has been so insignificant that the rule itself may be
regarded as of no practical account.

The foregoing Rules with the Table were laid before Parliament in the usual
way, and so received the required statutory sanction.

After 1894 steamers were built of a much larger tonnage than 10,000, the increase culminating in the "Titanic," with a gross tonnage of 46,328. As the vessels built increased in size, so one would have thought the necessity for increased lifeboat accommodation would grow; but the rules and table remained stationary, and nothing was done to them by way of change. The explanation of this long delay (from 1894-1912) was given before me by Sir Alfred Chalmers, who had Chalmers 22875 served under the Board of Trade as Nautical Advisor from 1896 to August, 1911. He is now retired. I think it will be well if I give his explanation in his own words. He says : " I considered the matter very closely from time to time. I first " of all considered the record of the trade—that is to say, the record of the casualties " —and to see what immunity from loss there was. I found it was the safest mode " of travel in the world, and I thought it was neither right nor the duty of a State " Department to impose regulations upon that mode of travel as long as the record " was a clean one. Secondly, I found that, as ships grew bigger, there were such " improvements made in their construction that they were stronger and better ships, " both from the point of view of watertight compartments and also absolute " strength, and I considered that that was the road along which the shipowners " were going to travel, and that they should not be interfered with. I then went " to the maximum that is down in the Table—16 boats and upwards, together with " the supplementary boats, and I considered from my experience that that was the " maximum number that could be rapidly dealt with at sea and that could be safely " housed without encumbering the vessel's decks unduly. In the next place, I con- " sidered that the traffic was very safe on account of the routes—the definite routes " being agreed upon by the different companies, which tended to lessen the risk of " collision, and to avoid ice and fog. Then, again, there was the question of wire- " less telegraphy, which had already come into force on board of these passenger " ships. I was seized of the fact that in July, 1901, the ' Lucania ' had been fitted " with wireless telegraphy, and the Cunard Line, generally, fitted it during that " year to all their ships. The Allan Line fitted it in 1902, and I am not sure that in " 1904 it had not become quite general on the trans-Atlantic ships. That, of course, " entered into my consideration as well. Then another point was the manning. It " was quite evident to me that if you went on crowding the ships with boats you " would require a crew which were not required otherwise for the safe navigation " of the ship, or for the proper upkeep of the ship, but you are providing a crew " which would be carried uselessly across the ocean, that never would be required " to man the boats. Then the last point, and not the least, was this, that the " voluntary action of the owners was carrying them beyond the requirements of our " scale, and when voluntary action on the part of shipowners is doing that, I think " that any State Department should hold its hand before it steps in to make a hard- " and-fast scale for that particular type of shipping. I considered that that scale " fitted all sizes of ships that were then afloat, and I did not consider it necessary " to increase it, and that was my advice to Sir Walter Howell."

I appreciate this explanation, and I think there is much force in it. At the same time, it seems to me that it does not justify the delay. Even taking all these matters into consideration, it cannot be that the provision for boat accommodation made in 1894 for vessels of 10,000 tons and upwards remained sufficient to 1910, when vessels of 45,000 tons were being built. Two considerations demonstrate this. The first is that some shipowners recognised the insufficiency of the require- ments of the Board of Trade, and voluntarily exceeded those requirements by pro- viding larger boat accommodation than the old rules and table exacted. The second is that shortly before Sir Alfred Chalmers left the Board of Trade, the Board had begun to direct attention to the amending of their rules in this connection.

It appears that in November, 1910, a question was asked in the House of 22755 Commons as to whether the attention of the President of the Board of Trade had been called to the fact that the "Olympic," a sister ship of the "Titanic," was provided with 14 lifeboats only. The answer given was that the "Olympic" (which was then in course of construction) would carry 14 lifeboats and two ordinary boats of an aggregate capacity of 9,752 cubic feet, which was in excess of the requirements of the statutory rules. On the 15th February, 1911, a further question was asked as to the date of the last regulations, and whether, having regard to the increased tonnage of modern ships, the desirability of revising the regulations would be considered by the Board of Trade. The answer by the President was : " Those regulations were last revised in " 1894. The question of their further revision is engaging the serious attention " of the Board of Trade, and I have decided to refer the matter to the Merchant

D

"Shipping Advisory Committee for consideration and advice." Three days afterwards, namely, on the 18th of February, 1911, a circular letter was sent out by the Board of Trade to the Board's principal officers at Liverpool, London and Glasgow, asking each of those gentlemen to draft such an extension of the existing boat scale as he might think satisfactory and reasonable for the conditions of large passenger steamers. This circular letter was answered by the principal officer in Glasgow (Mr. Harris) on the 24th February, 1911, by the principal officer in London (Mr. Park) on the 27th February, 1911, and by the principal officer in Liverpool (Mr. Young) on the 3rd March, 1911. It is sufficient to say of these answers that they all suggested a large extension of the statutory requirements.

Archer,
24246.

Meanwhile, namely, on the 28th February, 1911, Mr. Archer, the Board of Trade's principal ship surveyor, had also drawn up a scale. This was a more exacting scale than that of any of the three principal officers. By his scale a vessel of the tonnage of the "Titanic" would have had to carry boat accommodation equivalent to at least 24,937 cubic feet, which would have been sufficient to hold all, and more than all, the persons who were on board at the time of the disaster (2,201). It would not, however, have been nearly sufficient to have held all that the vessel might lawfully have carried, viz., 3,547, and it is to be observed with reference to Mr. Archer's scale that in it he suggests an extension of Rule 12, by which (if the vessel were divided into efficient watertight compartments) the total boat accommodation might be reduced much more than Rule 12 as it stands would permit. If this reduction be taken into account, the boat accommodation would fall so that it would be sufficient only for 1,750 persons. Mr. Archer's view was that shipowners should be encouraged to increase the flotability of the ships they built, and that the way to encourage them was to relax the legal requirements as to boats as their plans advanced in that direction. The great object was so to build the ship that in the event of a disaster she would be her own lifeboat.*

Having obtained these four reports, the Board of Trade, on the 4th April, 1911, submitted the matter to their Advisory Committee, and obtained the Committee's report on the 4th July, 1911. The following are copies (with omissions of immaterial passages) of the Board of Trade's letter of the 4th April, 1911, and of the Advisory Committee's report of the 4th July, 1911 :—

Board of Trade, Marine Department,
7, Whitehall Gardens, London, S.W.,
4th April, 1911.

SIR,

I am directed by the Board of Trade to enclose herewith, for the information of the Merchant Shipping Advisory Committee, a copy of a question asked in the House of Commons on the 15th February and of the answer given by the President of the Board of Trade with reference to the Life-Saving Appliances Rules made under section 427 of the Merchant Shipping Act, 1894.

The Board are of opinion that the Table in the Appendix to the Rules should be extended upwards in the form indicated in the accompanying scale, so as to provide for vessels of tonnage up to 50,000 tons gross and upwards.

It appears to the Board that the number of boats and the boat capacity need not necessarily increase in a regular proportion according to the increase in tonnage, and that due regard should be paid to what is reasonable and practicable in passenger steamers exceeding 10,000 tons. . . . . .

I am to state that the Board would be obliged if the Merchant Shipping Advisory Committee would be so good as to suggest in what manner the scale (*see* accompanying copy) should be continued upwards having due regard to the considerations indicated above.

I am further to state that the Board would be glad to learn whether the Advisory Committee are of opinion that Rule 12 should or should not be revised so as to exempt altogether from the requirement of additional boats and/or rafts those vessels which are divided into efficient watertight compartments to the satisfaction of the Board of Trade. . . . . . .

I am, etc,

The Secretary,   (Signed)   WALTER J. HOWELL.
    Merchant Shipping
       Advisory Committee.

MERCHANT SHIPPING ADVISORY COMMITTEE.

SIR   4th July, 1911.

WE have the honour to report that your letter of the 4th April with reference to the minimum number of lifeboats to be carried on vessels of 10,000 tons gross tonnage and upwards, and your letter of the 17th May on the subject of the depth of lifeboats, have been very carefully considered by the Merchant Shipping Advisory Committee, and that it was unanimously decided at a meeting held on the 29th ultimo to adopt the report of a Sub-Committee which was specially appointed to inquire into these questions.

Archer,
24256

---

* It may be mentioned that Mr. Archer stated in the witness-box that since the disaster to the "Titanic" he had modified his views and thought that Rule 12 should be discontinued.

A copy of the report is accordingly forwarded herewith, and the Committee desire us to suggest for the consideration of the Board of Trade, that effect should be given to the recommendations contained in it.

We are, &c.,

(Signed) NORMAN HILL,
Chairman.

(Signed) R. W. MATTHEW,
Secretary.

Sir Walter J. Howell,
Assistant Secretary,
Marine Department,
Board of Trade.

Report of the Life-Saving Appliances Sub-Committee to the Merchant Shipping Advisory Committee.

In accordance with the decision of the Merchant Shipping Advisory Committee at their meeting on Friday, the 28th April, we have given careful consideration to the letter of the 4th April from the Board of Trade, in which the Committee were asked to advise :—

(1) as to the manner in which the table in the Appendix to the Life Saving Appliances Rules should be extended so as to provide for vessels of tonnage up to 50,000 tons gross and upwards ; and

(2) as to whether Rule 12 should, or should not, be revised so as to exempt altogether from the requirement of additional boats and/or rafts, those vessels which are divided into efficient water-tight compartments to the satisfaction of the Board of Trade.

In considering these questions, we have had specially in mind the fact that the number of passengers carried does not necessarily increase in proportion to the increase in the tonnage of the vessel.   This is particularly true in the case of vessels exceeding 10,000 tons, a type of vessel which is practically only built to provide special accommodation for large numbers of first and second class passengers.

Similarly there is no fixed relation between the tonnage of vessels and the deck space available for the carrying of lifeboats under davits.   Increase in the length of a vessel is only one of the factors, and often not the most material factor contributing to the increase in its tonnage, and it should also be remembered, in estimating the space available for the launching of lifeboats, that it is impossible to place davits forward of the bridge, and very undesirable to have them on the quarters of the vessel.

We are strongly of opinion that every encouragement should be given to secure the provision of vessels which by their construction have been rendered as unsinkable as possible, and which are provided with efficient means for communicating with the shore or with other vessels in case of disaster.

In view of these considerations, we have agreed upon the following recommendations :—

1. That it is questionable whether it is practicable to increase the number of davits ;

2. That any increase in the number of lifeboats to be carried can probably be best effected by providing for the launching of further boats from the existing davits ;

3. That the table should be extended in the manner indicated below, viz. :—

Gross Tonnage.	Minimum Number of Boats to be placed under Davits.	Minimum Number of Additional Boats to be readily available for Attachment to Davits.	Total Minimum Cubic Contents of Boats required by Columns 2 and 3.
(1)	(2)	(3)	(4)
			Cubic Feet.
10,000 and under 12,000 ...	16	—	5,500
12,000 and under 20,000 ...	16	2	6,200
20,000 and under 35,000 ...	16	4	6,900
35,000 and under 45,000 ...	16	6	7,600
45,000 and upwards... ...	16	8	8,300

It is further recommended that all passenger vessels of 10,000 tons gross tonnage and upwards should be required to be fitted with wireless telegraphy apparatus ;

4. That the Rules should be amended so as to admit of decked lifeboats of an approved type being stowed on top of one another or under an open lifeboat, subject to suitable arrangements being made for launching promptly the boats so stowed ;

5. That the additional boats and rafts required under the provisions of Division A, Class 1 (*d*) of the Life-Saving Appliances Rules shall be of at least such carrying capacity that they, and the boats required by columns 2 and 3 of the above Table, provide together three-fourths more than the minimum cubic contents required by column 4 of that Table ;

6. That vessels divided into efficient water-tight compartments to the satisfaction of the Board of Trade should (provided they are fitted with wireless telegraphy apparatus) be exempt from the requirement of additional boats and/or rafts.   The Committee suggest, in this connection, that the Board of Trade should review the requirements designed to attain the standards as to water-tight compartments at present enforced by them under Rule 12,

having regard to the developments of shipbuilding since the report of the Committee on the spacing and construction of watertight bulkheads.

We have also had before us the Board's further letter of the 17th May enquiring whether, in the opinion of the Advisory Committee, it would be advisable to prescribe a maximum depth for lifeboats as compared with their breadth, and, if so, what that proportion should be.

In connection with this letter, we have been supplied by the Board of Trade with reports from their principal officers in Great Britain, giving the dimensions and cubic capacities of the various kinds of boats on five typical ships in each of eight ports.

We recommend that the Board should be advised to alter the Life Saving Appliances Rules so as to provide that, in future, the depth of lifeboats supplied to a British merchant vessel shall not exceed 44 per cent. of their breadth.

(Signed)   NORMAN HILL.
A. M. CARLISLE.
S. CROSS.
WM. THEODORE DOXFORD.
GEO. N. HAMPSON.
ROBERT A. OGILVIE.
T. ROYDEN.
T. ROME.
THOMAS SPENCER.
J. HAVELOCK WILSON.

It will be observed that if effect had been given by the Board of Trade to the Report of the Advisory Committee the requirements for a vessel of the size of the "Titanic" would have reached 14,525 cubic feet (8,300 plus $\frac{3}{4}$ths of 8,300, namely, 6,225), with, however, this qualification that if the vessel were divided into efficient watertight compartments (as she probably was) and fitted with wireless telegraphy (as she certainly was) a provision of a boat capacity of 8,300 cubic feet, equivalent to space for 830 persons, would have been legally sufficient. This would have been much less than the accommodation with which the "Titanic" when she put to sea was, in fact, provided (namely for 1,178 persons).

Effect, however, was not given to the report. A question arose with reference to the dimensions of lifeboats, and it was thought better to get that question settled before proceeding to revise the rules. The examination of this question involved making several experiments which caused delay : and it was not until the 16th April, 1912, that a reply was sent by the Board of Trade to the Advisory Committee. It will be noticed that the date of this reply is just after the disaster to the "Titanic" became known. I am, however, quite satisfied that instructions for the preparation of this letter had been given in the offices of the Board of Trade some days before the 16th, and that the letter was not sent in consequence of the disaster. It is desirable to set it out.

Board of Trade, Marine Department,
7, Whitehall Gardens, London, S.W., 16th April 1912.

SIR,

WITH reference to your letter of the 4th July last respecting certain questions raised in connection with the proposed revision of the Life Saving Appliances Rules, I am directed by the Board of Trade to state, for the information of the Advisory Committee, that they have given very careful consideration to the report of the Life Saving Appliances Sub-Committee which was forwarded with your letter.

As regards the recommendations with reference to the proposed extension of the Table (Appendix to the Life Saving Appliances Rules) showing the minimum number of boats to be placed under davits, the Board are glad to observe that the Committee agree that alterations and additions are now necessary to meet the changed conditions due to recent developments in the size of passenger steamships and in the number of persons which these vessels can accommodate.

The Board of Trade note that the gradations of tonnage in the extension of the scale suggested by the Advisory Committee are not the same as those in the form of scale submitted to them by the Board ; while the increase in the number of boats is not in the number to be placed under davits, but in the number of additional boats required to be readily available for attachment to davits. It is observed that the Committee hold the view that " it is questionable whether it is practicable to increase the number of davits," and " that any increase in the number of lifeboats to be carried can " probably be best effected by providing for the launching of further boats from the existing davits."

The Board presume that, in arriving at these conclusions, the Committee have had regard to ships already built rather than to new ships, as they see no reason why there would be any difficulty in having more than eight pairs of davits on each side of the ship, provided that the requirements of Life Saving Appliances rules were known before the plans were prepared.

The Board are of opinion that a very careful and thorough revision of the table should now be made, and I am to transmit herewith a copy of a memorandum and tables prepared by the Professional Adviser to the Marine Department, containing a full and considered opinion on the subject of the extension of the boat scale and cognate questions.

As regards the proposed amendment of the Rules, so as to admit of decked lifeboats of an approved type being stowed one above another, or under an open lifeboat, I am to state that this question is now under consideration, and a communication will be addressed to you shortly on the subject.

With reference to the Advisory Committee's recommendation regarding the amendment of Rule 12 of the General Rules, the Board desire me to state that the questions raised in the recommendation are of wide application, and of such importance that the Board do not think that they can be adequately considered except by a Committee of equal standing to the Committee which reported in 1891 on the Spacing and Construction of Watertight Bulkheads in the Mercantile Marine. The Board have the question of the appointment of a Committee under consideration.

In connection with the Advisory Committee's recommendation that the depth of lifeboats shall not exceed 44 per cent. of their breadth, I am to transmit herewith, for their consideration, a draft amendment of Rules Nos. 1, 2, and 3 of the General Rules with reference to the construction of ships' boats.

The Board have made full inquiry into the question of the construction of ships' boats, and obtained some useful information as to the average depth of boat which is deemed desirable for safety and utility, and the ratio of that depth to the breadth, and they attach so much importance to this element of boat construction that they think it should receive the careful attention of the Committee. The Board think that the Committee, in the light of this additional information, may reconsider the opinions expressed on this point in their letter of the 4th July.

I am therefore to transmit herewith copies of memoranda by the Professional Adviser to the Marine Department and the acting Principal Ship Surveyor.

The Board desire me to state that they would be glad to be furnished with the Advisory Committee's views as to the application of the proposed new rules and boat scale, e.g., whether they should apply to ships already built, and if so, to what extent. They regard it as of great importance, on the one hand, that all British vessels should be provided with a proper and sufficient equipment of life-saving appliances, and, on the other, that regulations should not be enforced without notice which would necessitate important structural alterations and consequent heavy expense in vessels already built.

I am to add that in order to make the constitution of the Committee, when considering this question, agree with that of the Statutory Life-Saving Appliances Committee indicated in the Seventeenth Schedule to the Merchant Shipping Act, 1894, the Board have followed the course adopted on previous occasions, and have invited Lloyd's Register of British and Foreign Shipping and the Institute of London Underwriters to select a representative who will be available to sit on the Advisory Committee when the question is under consideration.

I am, &c.,
(Signed)   WALTER J. HOWELL.

The Secretary,
    Merchant Shipping
        Advisory Committee,
            7, Whitehall Gardens, S.W.

Extension of Life-Saving Apparatus Tables.

It will be seen that I have given priority in importance to the form of ships' boats rather than to their number on the principle that a few reliable boats are of greater value than a large number of indifferent ones ; but if the former desirable condition can be obtained by the proposed alterations in our rules as to measurement, &c., we are freer to approach the question of adding to the number of boats provided for in the existing tables.

As with the question of ratio D : B dealt with by the Advisory Committee last year, so with the question of boat increase and relative increase of cubic capacity dealt with by them on the same occasion, perhaps the Board might inform the Committee that they are not satisfied that a slightly different recommendation might not have been made had the matter been still further considered at the time.

Referring to the table of boat capacities computed by them particularly it might be helpful if the Board laid before them for consideration the table, which I attach hereto and submit, as showing a more reasonable proportionate increase in capacity than appears so far, in my opinion, in the other papers before us. It will be seen in this statement that the number of boats recommended by the Advisory Committee is practically retained, but the unit of increase in capacity is put at 300 cubic feet.

Perhaps I should state here what actuated me in fixing upon this rate of increase. I realised that in all probability it would become the practice on these large liners to provide boats under davits which would contain the entire cubic feet required by the L.S.A. Rules, that is—the quantity required by rule under davits plus the addition of $\frac{3}{4}$ths and it occurred to me that if, after the figure 5,500 cubic feet the increase of capacity were uniform and moderate it would result in a total at $1\frac{3}{4}$ which would by incidence fit in with the scale of boats already recommended as requisite in the Report of the Advisory Committee and in my own, i.e., assuming that the boats are of 500 cubic feet. *Example :* take a vessel of 30,000 tons and under 35,000 tons, according to the table I submit she would be required to have by the $1\frac{3}{4}$ rule a total boat capacity of 12,250 cubic feet which at 500 cubic feet per boat equals 24 boats nearly. There should be no difficulty on the large ships in carrying this quantity under davits, i.e., 18 directly under davits and six boats inboard.

Please see incidental table attached.

A. H. Y.
28.3.12.

(Mr. A. H. Young, Professional Adviser of the Board of Trade.)

Proposed Extension of Boat Scale.

Gross Tons.			Boats.	Minimum Total Cubic Contents of Boats required to be carried under Davits.
10,000 and under 12,000	...	...	16	5,500 c. ft.
12,000 „ 15,000	...	...	18	5,800 c. ft.
15,000 „ 20,000	...	...	20	6,100 c. ft.
20,000 „ 25,030	...	...	22	6,400 c. ft.
25,000 „ 30,000	...	...	24	6,700 c. ft.
30,000 „ 35,000	...	...	24	7,000 c. ft.
35,000 „ 40,000	...	...	24	7·300 c. ft.
40,000 „ 45,000	...	...	24	7,600 c. ft.
45,000 „ 50,000	...	...	26	7,900 c. ft.
50,000 and upwards ...	...	...	26	8,200 c. ft.

Please see the accompanying incidental table showing how this number of boats can provide for the three-quarters additional capacity also, if of about 500 cubic ft. per boat to 600 cubic ft.

A. H. Y.

Table of incidence (informative).

Gross Tons.	Number of Boats.	Cubic Feet.	Cubic Feet Additional.	Total Cubic Feet at 1¾.	Equivalent Boats.	
					At 500 Cu. Ft.	At 600 Cu. Ft.
10,000 and under 12,000	16	5,500	4,125	9,625	19 say or	16
12,000 „ „ 15,000	18	5,800	4,350	10,150	20 „ „	16
15,000 „ „ 20,000	20	6,100	4,575	10,675	21 „ „	18
20,000 „ „ 25,000	22	6,400	4,800	11,200	22 „ „	19
25,000 „ „ 30,000	24	6,700	5,025	11,725	24 „ „	20
30,000 „ „ 35,000	24	7,000	5,250	12,250	24 „ „	20
35,000 „ „ 40,000	24	7,300	5,475	12,775	25 „ „	21
40,000 „ „ 45,000	24	7,600	5,700	13,300	26 „ „	22
45,000 „ „ 50,000	26	7,900	5,925	13,825	27 „ „	23
50,000 and upwards ...	26	8,200	6,150	14,350	28 „ „	24

One-fourth of the above boats may be carried inboard, but they should not exceed 500 cubic ft. in capacity, so that they may be readily drawn up to the davits.

A. H. Y.
30.3.12.

Draft Amendment of General Rules.

(1) *Boats.*—All boats shall be constructed and properly equipped as provided by these rules, and shall be of such form and proportions that they shall have sufficient freeboard, and ample stability in a sea-way, when loaded with their full complement of persons and equipment.

All thwart and side seats must be fitted as low in the boat as practicable, and bottom boards must be fitted so that the thwarts shall not be more than 2 ft. 9 in. above them.

All boats and other life-saving appliances are to be kept ready for use to the satisfaction of the Board of Trade. Internal buoyancy apparatus may be constructed of wood, or of copper or yellow metal of not less than 18 oz. to the superficial foot, or of other durable material.

Section (A). A boat of this section shall be a lifeboat of whale-boat form, properly constructed of wood or metal, having for every 10 cubic ft. of her capacity, computed as in Rule (2), at least 1 cubic ft. of strong and serviceable inclosed air-tight compartments, so constructed that water cannot find its way into them. In the case of metal boats an addition will have to be made to the cubic capacity of the air-tight compartments, so as to give them buoyancy equal to that of the wooden boat.

Section (B). A boat of this section shall be a lifeboat, of whaleboat form, properly constructed of wood or metal, having inside and outside buoyancy apparatus together equal in efficiency to the buoyancy apparatus provided for a boat of section (A). At least one-half of the buoyancy apparatus must be attached to the outside of the boat.

Section (C). A boat of this section shall be a lifeboat, properly constructed of wood or metal, having some buoyancy apparatus attached to the inside and (or) outside of the boat, equal in efficiency to one-half of the buoyancy apparatus provided for a boat of section (A) or section (B). At least one-half of the buoyancy apparatus must be attached to the outside of the boat.

Section (D). A boat of this section shall be a properly constructed boat of wood or metal.

Section (E). A boat of this section shall be a boat of approved construction, form, and material, and may be collapsible.

(2) *Cubic Capacity.*—The cubic capacity of an open boat, and of a deck boat of section (D) or section (E) shall be ascertained by multiplying the product of the length, breadth, and depth by ·6, subject, however, to the following provisions:—

The length shall be measured from the foreside of the rabbet on the stem to the afterside of the rabbet on the stern post, and the breadth shall be measured from the outside of plank to the outside of plank amidships. The actual depth shall be measured from the top of the gunwale to the top of the bottom plank next to the keel, but the depth used in calculating the cubic capacity shall not in any case exceed 3·6 ft.; and if the actual depth measured is equal to or less than 3·6 ft., the depth used in calculating the cubic capacity shall not exceed 45 per cent. of the breadth measured as indicated above.

If the oars are pulled in rowlocks, the bottom of the rowlock is to be considered as the gunwale in measuring the depth of the boat.

If any question is raised requiring absolute accuracy, the cubic capacity of a boat shall be ascertained by Stirling's rule; subject to the foregoing provisions as to depth.

(3) *Number of Persons for Boats.*—(A) Subject to the provisions of paragraphs (*b*), (*c*), and (*d*) of this clause the number of persons* an open boat of section (A) shall be deemed fit to carry shall be the number of cubic feet ascertained as in Rule (2) divided by 10, and the number of persons* an open boat of section (B) or section (C), or an open or decked boat of section (D) or section (E) shall be deemed fit to carry shall be the number of cubic feet ascertained as in Rule (2) divided by 8. The space in the boat shall be sufficient for the seating of the persons carried in it, and for the proper use of the oars.

(*B*)—An open boat of section (A) or section (B) or section (C) or section (D) or section (E), shall not be deemed to be fit to carry the number of persons ascertained as in paragraph (A) of this clause unless the boat is so constructed that it has a mean sheer of at least half an inch for each foot of its length, and that the boat's half-girth amidships measured outside the planking from the side of the keel to the top of the gunwale is at least equal to nine-tenths of the sum of the boat's depth inside and half its maximum breadth amidships, and that the mean of the half-girths measured in the same manner at two points, one-quarter of the length of the boat from the stem and stern-post respectively, is at least equal to eight-tenths of the sum of the depth inside and half the maximum breadth amidships.

(*C*)—A decked boat of section (D) or section (E) shall not be deemed to be fit to carry the number of persons ascertained as in paragraph (A) of this clause, unless the top of the deck amidships is at a height above the water approved by the Board of Trade, when the boat is so loaded.

(*D*)—If the surveyor is doubtful as to the number of persons any open or decked boat is fit to carry, he may require the boat to be tested afloat with the intended number of persons on board.

(*E*)—The rules Numbers 1, 2, and 3, as now amended, are not to be retrospective, and are to apply only to boats built after

Ship's Boats.

The salient feature of the Reports of the Board's officers on this subject is the consensus of opinion that the form of a boat is the chief factor to be considered in determining its value as a life-saving appliance.

It has been found that while there are many boats of good form supplied to ships, there is yet a large proportion where the boats are not only not so good, but which can only be regarded as unsafe if they had on board anything approaching the number of persons for which they measure.

It is the latter type we are chiefly concerned with; how is it that the form has so deteriorated as to create this concern in our minds? I think the cause is not far to seek; it appears to be the outcome of (1) the shipowner's desire to carry the maximum number of persons in the minimum number of boats; (2) in the efforts of the shipbuilder, as a rule, to carry out the specification in which he has contracted to supply the owners with boats at a price, often very low, and naturally he does not sublet his contract with the boatbuilder at a loss; (3) the aim of the competing boatbuilder, which is to build his boats at as little cost price as possible, and yet to provide accommodation for the prescribed number of persons. He is probably limited as to length, and therefore relies on the breadth and depth; in this direction, he is unintentionally assisted by the Board's rule for measurement, viz., $\dfrac{\text{L} \times \text{B} \times \text{D} \times ·6}{10}$ or 8; so long, therefore, as he can obtain his breadth at one point for measurement purposes, it is quite immaterial to him how soon he fines away to the ends, with the result that the stability of the boat becomes almost entirely dependent upon the form of a very limited midship section, or the still smaller proportion of same that would be under water when in the loaded condition.

The boatbuilder may be further restricted as to breadth, and, therefore, he again detracts from the form a boat should have by dispensing with sheer and increasing the depth from

---

* See Rule of 14,6,11,

keel to gunwale amidships. This method of building boats enables him to obtain the capacity required by the owner at the expense of the boat's stability and utility.

No doubt when the Life-Saving Appliances Rules came into being, the divisors 10 and 8 for the different sections were deemed safe on the supposition that the usual full form of boat would not be largely departed from; experience has shown, however, that form is frequently sacrificed for the unworthy objects referred to above, and it follows, therefore, that either the form should be improved or a heavier divisor laid down.

It would, I think, be more effective to deal with form, and devise a rule by which we can ensure that a boat will be reasonably safe with its load, not merely in smooth water—as in our recent test—but in a sea-way. It is essential, therefore, to draw the attention of the Advisory Committee to the value the Board attach to form, and particularly to that part of it under water, emphasising the great necessity there is for an increase to the bearing surface of the under-water portion of boats, and this end can, no doubt, be best attained by the putting into practice of the suggestions made by the Principal Ship Surveyor for amending the rules, and which aim at prolonging the form or fulness of dimension of the midship body under-water well towards the ends of the boat. It is well known that by extending the body in this way greater buoyancy and stability are secured without materially affecting the speed. It is often supposed that defective stability due to bad form can be rectified by the disposition of the persons or things, but anyone with real experience of boats in a sea-way cannot fail to realise that this is the wrong principle to work on; granted, therefore, that the question of form must take priority—how can it be best attained? and if we refer to Mr. Archer's method of measurement, as stated in his amendment to the Rules, it will be seen how simple and effective it is. For the purpose of illustration we might take the model of a ship's boat obtained through the Board's surveyors at Glasgow, the dimensions of which enlarged to scale represent a boat of $\underset{30{\cdot}0\times8{\cdot}5\times3{\cdot}5}{\overset{\text{L}\quad\text{B}\quad\text{D}}{}}$ and is an embodiment of the proportions amidships and at quarter distance from each end, proposed by Mr. Archer.

It cannot be too strongly urged that for a ship's lifeboat to be fit to carry the number of persons it measures for in any degree of safety, whenever it may be required at sea, the under-water or bearing surface should be carried out to the ends as much as possible and all straight lines avoided. The bows of many of the existing types of boat are examples of the worst possible form for safety, and the counters are as bad—if they can be said to have *any*.

Depth.—It appears from the reports that the most generally approved ratio of depth to the breadth is $\frac{4}{10}$. This has been established, not only by our long experience, but by the numerous tests recently conducted by the Board's surveyors at various ports, and the attention of the Advisory Committee might be drawn to this fact.

It is, of course, necessary also to have a good free-board, but a well-proportioned boat does not require so much free-board as the commoner type, as with proper sheer and under-water surface she is easy in a sea-way. If the gunwale is too high there is loss of power over the oars, which is serious when for the safety of the boat she is required to be kept head-on to sea, and with a fresh breeze, even in a good boat, this is not always an easy matter.

It is matter for consideration that at the tests made by our surveyors the conditions were most favourable, being usually in smooth water of a sheltered dock, and, in not a few instances, considerable anxiety was felt for the safety of those on board when crowded in accordance to the existing rules. If it was thus in smooth water one dare hardly contemplate the results in a sea-way. If the shipowner does not see to it that a safe type of boat is provided, then the number of persons to be accommodated in boats which do not come up to the proportions deemed safe by the Board of Trade should be very considerably **curtailed.**

A. H. Y.,
23.3.12.

Construction of Ship's Boats.

It will, I think, be useful to consider the principal factors that govern the dimensions of boats forming part of the life-saving apparatus in merchant ships.

The minimum number and capacity of boats are determined by the regulations, and the capacity is determined by the product of the length, breadth, and depth of the boats. As the space on the ship in which to stow the boats is generally limited, it is generally found easier to increase their depth than the length or breadth, and this is further encouraged, I believe, by the cost of boats being quoted at so much per foot in length. The builder or owner determines the dimensions of the boat; the boatbuilder is concerned merely with the construction and, in most cases, usually their form or lines.

Attention has been called by the Mark Lane Surveyors to the form and proportions of the boats used in the Royal Navy. The proportion of depth to breadth is greater than is apparent from the particulars given, as all boats larger than a 30-ft. gig have $6\frac{1}{2}$-in. washboards above the gunwale, and even the gigs and many of the smaller boats have portable washboards. It must also be remembered that all the navy boats are square-sterned, except the whaleboat, and are designed with easy lines so as to make good sailers, no air cases are fitted, and the seats are kept very low. The boats are not provided simply as life-saving appliances; as a matter of fact the life-saving equipment of a warship is extremely small.

It is true that each type of boat is given a certain "life-saving capacity," which is ascertained by crowding in as many men as practicable with boat in still water and all equipment on board. This number agrees closely with that obtained by the Board's rule $\dfrac{L \times B \times D \times \cdot 6}{8}$. These boats, moreover, have a much smaller freeboard than is considered desirable in the merchant navy; but the occupants are all under discipline and in charge of experienced seamen. In the mercantile marine it may, and often does, happen, that the boats are crowded with panic-stricken men, women, and children, and instances have occurred, I believe, wherein there has not been a single man in the boat who has ever handled an oar before. Having these points in view, I do not agree that the navy type of boat is the most suitable for our purpose.

The chief desiderata in a ship's boat as a life-saving appliance are—

(1) To carry the maximum number of people without overcrowding; and with
(2) A reasonable amount of stability and freeboard;
(3) And without undue interference with the use of oars.

(1) is almost wholly dependent on the length and breadth of the boat; provided (2) is satisfied; depth has very little influence on it. For example, take a boat $30 \times 9 \times 3 \cdot 5$, 567 cubic ft. by our rule, as a section (D) or (E) boat it should carry $\dfrac{567}{8} = 72$ people; such a boat should allow $\dfrac{30 \times 9 \times 8}{72} = 3$ sq. ft. of area per person at the gunwale, which should be ample if all sit in the bottom who cannot find seating room on the side benches or thwarts.

(2) Stability and freeboard are dependent upon the boat's breadth, depth, and form. The element of length does not enter into it, and it would be most unreasonable to limit the ratio of length to breadth, as suggested from Liverpool, or to limit the depth to the cube root of the length, as proposed by one of the London surveyors. Mr. Gemmell gives particulars, M. 26,298, of four boats tested, which proved to have ample accommodation and stability for the complements allowed by the regulations; the ratio of depth to breadth varied from ·41 to ·45.

Captain O'Sullivan also reported five boats which he tested with ratios of D to B, varying from ·4 to ·44, all except one being satisfactory, the exception being rather tender and overcrowded, due to poor lines. The freeboards of all these boats when loaded were, I think, sufficient. The depth in no case exceeded 3·6, and only in one case did the ratio exceed ·44.

The Surveyors, Liverpool, tested a boat 3·75 deep and having a ratio of $D/b = \cdot 41$, which proved satisfactory.

Captain Griffiths tested a boat 4·1 deep, having a ratio $D/b = \cdot 455$, which he considered to be unsafe with the full complement on board.

The consensus of opinion is that the depth should not exceed 3 ft. 5 in. or 3 ft. 6 in., and the ratio of D/b should not exceed ·44. This, however, is not sufficient to guarantee sufficient seating and stability. Captain Clarke tested a boat 24·4 × 6·55 × 2·45, which was very unsafe with the rule complement on board. The ratio D/b is only ·38 in this case, It will be seen, however, that this craft has exceptionally fine lines and is evidently quite unsuited to carry the rule complement. It is quite evident that the form of the boat must be taken into account.

The dimensions of boats vary so greatly that generally the boatbuilder builds his boats "to the eye," using only a midship mould; it follows that the forms of boats of the same dimensions will vary considerably and with different workmen. Something more is required than a limitation in the ratio of depth to breadth. It is desirable that the sheer should be ample, and the form not unduly fined away within the midship half length. From consideration of the particulars and lines of the boats mentioned in the surveyor's reports, I think a simple rule to regulate the form may be devised such as I will indicate later.

It is, I think, necessary to limit the depth as a factor for ascertaining the number to be accommodated. The increase of depth beyond a certain point, while unduly increasing the number of people that may be carried, increases proportionately the required air case capacity, to meet which the seats have to be raised with a corresponding increase in the height of the centre of gravity and decrease in the stability and difficulty in rowing. A boat 3·6 deep would have the thwarts about 3 ft. above the bottom, and any increase in this height makes it very difficult for any ordinary man to row when sitting down. In rough sea the men would have very little control over the oars if standing up. A further objection to the very deep boat is its small stability in the light condition. It is not, I believe, an unusual occurrence for such boats to capsize in rough weather, before the passengers or crew can be got into them, and I have myself seen such a boat capsize in dock with only two men in it; due to lumpy water and a stiff breeze catching it on the beam when coming out of the shelter afforded by the dock wall.

I do not think, however, any limit of depth should be imposed, except as a measure of capacity. Any rules that may be devised should be such as are of easy and ready application, and which will not bear harshly on the boats that have already been accepted. I therefore suggest that the present rules will sufficiently meet the case, with the following modification.

In no case should the depth to be used in General Rule (2) exceed 3·6 ft. and 45 per cent. of the breadth. In all cases where the actual depth is 45 per cent. of the breadth or less, the maximum number of persons, as ascertained by Rule (3) should not be allowed unless the boat has been found capable of carrying that number by actual test in the water, or unless the boat has at least $\frac{1}{2}$ in. of sheer per foot of length, and the half-girth amidships, measured outside the plank, from the side of the keel to the top of the gunwale, is at least 90 per cent. of the sum of the depth and the half breadth, and the mean of the half girths as similarly measured at one quarter the boat's length from the stem and stern post are at least 80 per cent. of the sum of the midship depth and half breadth.

The thwarts and side benches should be kept as low as practicable, and the bottom boards should be so fitted that the height of the thwarts above them will not exceed 2 ft. 9 in.

(Intd.) A. J. D.,

27.1.12.

(Mr. A. J. Daniel, Acting Principal Ship Surveyor
to the Board of Trade.)

It should be stated that the new Committee on Bulkheads mentioned in the paragraph of this letter which deals with Rule 12 has now been formed.

Subsequently Sir Walter Howell wrote and sent three letters to the Advisory Committee which were as follows:—

Board of Trade, Marine Department,
7, Whitehall Gardens, London, S.W.,
20th April, 1912.

Immediate.

SIR,

WITH reference to previous correspondence between the Department and your Committee respecting the revision of the statutory rules for Life-Saving Appliances on British ships, and particularly to the letter from this Department of the 16th April, I am directed by the Board of Trade to state that as an entirely new situation has been created by the recent disaster to the s.s. "Titanic" they assume that the Committee, in reconsidering the matter in connection with the suggestions already put before them by the Board will have full regard to this new situation, and the facts of the disaster so far as ascertained.

As you are doubtless aware, suggestions have been made in the House of Commons and elsewhere to the effect that, in view of the loss of the "Titanic," action should be taken by the Board of Trade in regard to certain questions other than those expressly dealt with in the Life-Saving Appliances Rules, e.g., in regard to (1) steamship routes in the North Atlantic; (2) the speed of steamers where there may be dangers to navigation; and (3) the provision and use of searchlights on large passenger steamers; and the Board would be glad to know the Committee's views in regard to these, and any other suggestions which may have come to their knowledge, intended to diminish the risk, or to mitigate the effects of accidents to passenger vessels at sea.

I am, &c.,
(Signed)   WALTER J. HOWELL.

The Secretary,
Merchant Shipping Advisory Committee.

Board of Trade, Marine Department,
7, Whitehall Gardens, London, S.W.,
24th April, 1912.

SIR,

WITH reference to previous correspondence between this Department and your Committee respecting the revision of the statutory rules for life-saving appliances on British ships, and particularly to the letter from this Department of the 16th April, in which you were informed that the question of the proposed amendment of the rules so as to admit of decked lifeboats being stowed one above another or one under an open lifeboat, was under consideration, I am directed by the Board of Trade to state, for the information of your Committee, that the Board of Trade will be glad if the Committee will consider whether any, and if so what, amendments of the rules, and in particular of the rule of the 19th April, 1910, and the rule of the 14th June, 1911, are in their opinion desirable with the object of supplementing the boats immediately under davits by as much additional boat accommodation as is practicable, having regard to the new situation which has been created by the recent disaster to the s.s. "Titanic."

A plan illustrating the principle is being prepared so as to be in readiness for your Committee by Friday.

I am, &c.,
(Signed)   WALTER J. HOWELL.

The Secretary,
Merchant Shipping Advisory Committee,

Board of Trade, Marine Department,
7, Whitehall Gardens, London, S.W.,
25th April, 1912.

Sir,

WITH reference to previous correspondence respecting the proposed revision of the statutory regulations as to boats and life-saving appliances on ships, I am directed by the Board of Trade to state, for the information of the Merchant Shipping Advisory Committee, that, apart from the questions which have been raised regarding the boat accommodation on vessels over 10,000 tons, it seems desirable to consider whether the provision of boats and other life-saving appliances required by the rules in the case of vessels under 10,000 tons is satisfactory, or whether the rules or the boat scale should be altered in respect of their application to such vessels; and the Board would be glad to be favoured with the observations of the Committee on this point in addition to those that have already been referred to them.

I am, &c.,

The Secretary,   (Signed)   WALTER J. HOWELL.
Merchant Shipping Advisory Committee.

To these letters the Advisory Committee sent the following answer :—

Merchant Shipping Advisory Committee,
7, Whitehall Gardens, London, S.W.,
27th April, 1912.

Sir,

WE are desired by the Merchant Shipping Advisory Committee to inform you that your letters of the 16th, 20th, 24th and 25th instant were brought before the Committee at a meeting held yesterday.

The Committee fully recognise that the proved impossibility of keeping such a vessel as the "Titanic" afloat after a collision with ice, until the arrival of outside succour, has created an entirely new situation which was neither in the contemplation of the Board of Trade nor of the Committee in the consideration of the extension of the existing boat scale in regard to vessels of 10,000 tons and upwards.

In advising on such extension in July last, the Committee aimed at providing ample boat accommodation on large passenger vessels in accordance with the principles that were adopted by the original Life-Saving Appliances Committee, and which principles had apparently been fully justified by many years of experience. It is with satisfaction that the Committee note that the Board of Trade, apart from the new possibilities demonstrated by the loss of the "Titanic," agreed in the essentials with the recommendation of the Committee.

In face of the new facts, the Committee at their meeting yesterday re-opened entirely the question of the revision of the boat scale for large passenger vessels with a view of providing the maximum of protection for the passengers and crew in the event of an overwhelming disaster, whilst, at the same time, maintaining the principles in regard to the stability and sea-going qualities of the ship itself, and to the prompt and efficient handling of the boats carried under the existing scale, which hitherto have proved not only essential to safety, but also adequate for all ordinary emergencies. The questions involved are not free from difficulty, but they will receive the immediate attention of the Committee. Pending their consideration, the Committee note that assurances have been received by the Board of Trade from representatives of most of the large passenger lines to the effect that every effort will be made to equip their vessels, at the earliest possible moment, with boats and rafts sufficient to accommodate all persons on board.

In regard to the recommendation forwarded with the Committee's letter of the 4th July last, that the Board of Trade should, having regard to the developments in shipbuilding since the Report of the Committee of 1891 on Spacing and Construction of Watertight Bulkheads, review the requirements designed to attain the standards at present enforced under Rule 12, the Advisory Committee note that the Board of Trade have under consideration the appointment of a Committee of equal standing to that of the Committee of 1891. In view of the great importance of this question the Advisory Committee desire us respectfully to urge that such a Committee be appointed at as early a date as possible.

The subject of the general revision of the statutory regulations as to boats and life-saving appliances on all ships, which, apart from the questions regarding the boat accommodation on vessels over 10,000 tons, is for the first time referred to the Advisory Committee by the letter of the 25th instant, together with the particular questions raised in the letters of the 16th, 20th, and 24th instant, are also receiving the immediate attention of the Committee.

At yesterday's meeting sub-committees were appointed to give immediate consideration to the subjects requiring detailed examination. These sub-committees will pursue their enquiries concurrently, and we are desired by the Advisory Committee to inform you that their investigation into the revision of the Life-Saving Appliances Rules will be proceeded with as expeditiously as possible.

We are, &c.,

(Signed)   NORMAN HILL,
Chairman.

Sir WALTER J. HOWELL, K.C.B.,
Assistant Secretary,   (Signed)   R. W. MATTHEW.
Marine Department,   Secretary.
Board of Trade.

This letter was acknowledged by the Board of Trade on the 10th May, 1912, as follows :—

Board of Trade, Marine Department,
7, Whitehall Gardens, London, S.W.,
10th May, 1912.

Sir,

    I am directed by the Board of Trade to acknowledge the receipt of, and to thank you for, your letter of the 27th April, stating that their letters of the 16th, 20th, 24th, and 25th April, have been considered by the Merchant Shipping Advisory Committee.

    The Board observe with satisfaction that, in view of the entirely new situation which has arisen, the Advisory Committee have decided to re-open the question of the revision of the Table in the Life-Saving Appliances Rules in so far as it governs the boat accommodation in vessels over 10,000 tons gross. The Board are further glad to observe that the question of a general revision of the Life-Saving Appliances Rules is also under consideration by the Committee, and in this connection they presume that, in considering the question of a general revision of the rules including the Table, the Committee will consider the principles on which the requirements as to boat accommodation should be based, including, *inter alia*, whether the Table should continue to be based on tonnage. Any conclusion reached by the Committee on this question would naturally affect the revision of the present Table as applying to vessels of more than 10,000 tons, upon which the Committee has already been engaged.

    The Board agree with the view expressed by the Advisory Committee that the appointment of another Committee on the Spacing and Construction of Watertight Bulkheads is desirable. Steps have already been taken by the President to form such a Committee, and he hopes to be able to announce the names within a few days. A further communication on this point will be addressed to the Committee in the course of a few days.

    The Board are glad to note that Sub-Committees have been appointed to deal concurrently with the subjects requiring detailed consideration in connection with the revision of the Life-Saving Appliances Rules.

    The Board desire me to add that they assume that the Committee, in considering the matters referred to them, will have regard to all important aspects of the question of Life-Saving Appliances, whether expressly dealt with in the Statutory Rules or not, and in particular to the essential question of the adequacy of the provision for lowering and manning the boats and rafts carried by vessels.

I am, &c.,
(Signed)   Walter J. Howell.

The Secretary,
Merchant Shipping Advisory Committee.
7, Whitehall Gardens, S.W.

    This finishes the history of the action of the Board of Trade in relation to the provision of boat accommodation on emigrant ships. The outstanding circumstance in it is the omission, during so many years, to revise the rules of 1894 and this, I think, was blameable, notwithstanding the excuse or explanation put forward by Sir Alfred Chalmers. I am, however, doubtful whether even if the rules had been revised, the change would have been such as to have required boat accommodation which would have increased the number of lives saved. Having regard to the recommendations of the Advisory Committee, the Board of Trade would probably not have felt justified in making rules which would have required more boat accommodation than that with which the "Titanic" was actually provided: and it is not to be forgotten that the "Titanic" boat accommodation was utilized to less than two-thirds of its capacity. These considerations, however, afford no excuse for the delay of the Board of Trade.

    The gross tonnage of a vessel is not, in my opinion, a satisfactory basis on which to calculate the provision of boat accommodation. Hitherto, I believe, it has been accepted as the best basis by all nations. But there seems much more to be said in favour of making the number of lives carried the basis and for providing boat or raft accommodation for all on board. Rule 12 of the Life Saving Appliances Rules of 1902, which deals with watertight compartments and boat accommodation, ought to be abolished. The provision of such compartments is of supreme importance but it is clear that it should not be sought at the expense of a decrease in boat accommodation. When naval architects have devised practical means for rendering ships unsinkable, the question of boat accommodation may have to be reconsidered, but until that time arrives boat accommodation should, where practicable, be carried for all on board. This suggestion may be thought by some to be extravagant. It has never been enforced in the mercantile marine of Great Britain, nor as far as I know in that of any foreign Nation. But it appears, nevertheless, to be admitted by all that it is possible without undue inconvenience or undue interference with commerce to increase considerably in many cases the accommodation hitherto carried and it seems, therefore, reasonable that the law should require an increase to be made. As far as foreign going passenger and emigrant steamships are concerned, I am of opinion that, unless justification be shown for deviating from this course, such ships should carry boats or rafts for all on board.

With reference to the second branch of the complaint against the Board of Trade, namely that their officials had failed to exercise due care in the supervision of the vessel's plans and in the inspection of the work done upon her, the charges broke down. Suggestions were made that the Board's requirements fell short of those of Lloyd's Registry ; but no evidence was forthcoming to support the suggestions. The investigation of the charges took much time, but it only served to show that the officials had discharged their duties carefully and well.

Powers of the Board of Trade as regards the supervision of designs of vessels.

The " Titanic " was efficiently designed and constructed to meet the contingencies which she was intended to meet.

The bulkheads were of ample strength. They were sufficiently closely spaced and were carried up in the vessel to a height greater than sufficient to meet the requirements of the 1891 Bulkheads Committee.

But I am advised that the ship could have been further subdivided so that she would probably have remained afloat longer than she did. The Board of Trade have, however, apparently no power to exercise any real supervision in the matter of sub-division. All they have express power to insist upon in this connection with respect to any steam vessel is that there shall be four watertight bulkheads—a provision quite inadequate for safety in a collision damaging the vessel abaft the collision bulkhead. They can also, if invited by the shipowner (but not otherwise), exercise supervision under Rule 12. This supervision I am told they have been invited to exercise in only 103 cases over a period of 18 years. In 69 of these cases the Board have expressed their satisfaction with the sub-division provided. It seems to me that the Board should be empowered to require the production of the designs of all passenger steamers at an early period of their construction and to direct such alterations as may appear to them to be necessary and practicable for the purpose of securing proper watertight sub-division.

FINDING OF THE COURT.

It is now convenient to answer the twenty-six questions submitted by the Board of Trade.

1. When the " Titanic " left Queenstown on or about 11th April last—
    (a) What was the total number of persons employed in any capacity on board her, and what were their respective ratings ?
    (b) What was the total number of her passengers, distinguishing sexes and classes, and discriminating between adults and children ?

Answer :

(a) The total number of persons employed in any capacity on board the " Titanic " was :

885

The respective ratings of these persons were as follows :—

Deck Department ...	...	...	66
Engine Department ...	...	...	325
Victualling Department	...	...	494
			885

N.B.—The eight bandsmen are not included in this number as their names appear in the 2nd Class Passenger List.

(b) The total number of passengers was 1,316. Of these :

			Male	Female	Total
1st Class	...	...	180	145	325
2nd Class	...	...	179	106	285
3rd Class	...	...	510	196	706
					1,316

Of the above, 6 children were in the 1st Class, 24 in the 2nd Class and 79 in the 3rd Class.   Total 109.

2. Before leaving Queenstown on or about 11th April last did the " Titanic " comply with the requirements of the Merchant Shipping Acts, 1894–1906, and the rules and regulations made thereunder with regard to the safety and otherwise of " passenger steamers " and " emigrant ships " ?

Answer :
Yes.

3. In the actual design and construction of the " Titanic " what special provisions were made for the safety of the vessel and the lives of those on board in the event of collisions and other casualties ?

Answer :
These have been already described.

4. (a) Was the " Titanic " sufficiently and efficiently officered and manned ? (b) Were the watches of the officers and crew usual and proper ?   (c) Was the " Titanic " supplied with proper charts ?

Answer :
    (a) Yes.
    (b) Yes.
    (c) Yes.

5. (a) What was the number of the boats of any kind on board the " Titanic " ? (b) Were the arrangements for manning and launching the boats on board the " Titanic " in case of emergency proper and sufficient ?   (c) Had a boat drill been held on board, and if so, when ?   (d) What was the carrying capacity of the respective boats ?

Answer :
    (a) 2 Emergency boats.
    14 Lifeboats.
    4 Engelhardt boats.

(b) No, but see page 38.

(c) No.

(d) The carrying capacity of the :

2 Emergency boats was for	80	persons.
14 Lifeboats was for	910	,,
4 Engelhardt boats was for	188	,,
or a total of	1,178	,,

6. (a) What installations for receiving and transmitting messages by wireless telegraphy were on board the " Titanic " ? (b) How many operators were employed on working such installations ? (c) Were the installations in good and effective working order, and were the number of operators sufficient to enable messages to be received and transmitted continuously by day and night ?

Answer :

(a) A Marconi 5 Kilowatt motor generator with two complete sets of apparatus supplied from the ship's dynamos, with an independent storage battery and coil for emergency, was fitted in a house on the Boat Deck.

(b) Two.

(c) Yes.

7. (a) At or prior to the sailing of the " Titanic " what, if any, instructions as to navigation were given to the master or known by him to apply to her voyage ? (b) Were such instructions, if any, safe, proper and adequate, having regard to the time of year and dangers likely to be encountered during the voyage ?

Answer :

(a) No special instructions were given, but he had general instructions contained in the book of Rules and Regulations supplied by the Company. (See p. 24.)

(b) Yes, but having regard to subsequent events they would have been better if a reference had been made to the course to be adopted in the event of reaching the region of ice.

8. (a) What was in fact the track taken by the " Titanic " in crossing the Atlantic Ocean ? (b). Did she keep to the track usually followed by liners on voyages from the United Kingdom to New York in the month of April ? (c) Are such tracks safe tracks at that time of the year ? (d) Had the master any, and, if so, what discretion as regards the track to be taken ?

Answer :

(a) The Outward Southern Track from Queenstown to New York, usually followed in April by large steam vessels. (See page 24.)

(b) Yes, with the exception that instead of altering her course on approaching the position 42° N. 47° W. she stood on on her previous course for some 10 miles further South West, turning to S. 86° W. true at 5.50 p.m.

(c) The Outward and Homeward bound Southern tracks were decided on as the outcome of many years' experience of the normal movement of ice. They were reasonably safe tracks for the time of year, provided, of course, that great caution and vigilance when crossing the ice region were observed.

(d) Yes. Captain Smith was not fettered by any orders to remain on the track should information as to the position of ice make it in his opinion undesirable to adhere to it. The fact, however, of Lane Routes having been laid down for the common safety of all, would necessarily influence him to keep on (or very near) the accepted route, unless circumstances as indicated above should induce him to deviate largely from it.

9. (a) After leaving Queenstown on or about the 11th April last did information reach the " Titanic " by wireless messages or otherwise by signals of the existence of ice in certain latitudes ? (b) If so, what were such messages or signals and when were they received, and in what position or positions was the ice reported to be, and was the ice reported in or near the track actually being followed by the " Titanic"? (c) Was her course altered in consequence of receiving such information, and, if so, in what way ? (d) What replies to such messages or signals did the " Titanic " send, and at what times ?

Answer :

(a) Yes.

(b) See particulars of ice messages already set out (pp. 26-28).

(c) No. Her course was altered as hereinbefore described, but not in consequence of the information received as to ice.

(d) The material answers were:—

At 12-55 p.m. ss. " Titanic." " To Commander, ' Baltic.' Thanks for your message and good wishes. Had fine weather since leaving. Smith."

At 1-26 p.m. ss. " Titanic." " To Captain, ' Caronia.' Thanks for message and information. Have had variable weather throughout. Smith."

10. (a) If at the times referred to in the last preceding question or later the " Titanic " was warned of or had reason to suppose she would encounter ice, at what time might she have reasonably expected to encounter it ? (b) Was a good and proper look-out for ice kept on board ? (c) Were any, and, if so, what directions given to vary the speed—if so, were they carried out ?

Answer :

(a) At, or even before, 9.30 p.m. ship's time, on the night of the disaster.

(b) No. The men in the crow's nest were warned at 9-30 p.m. to keep a sharp look-out for ice ; the officer of the watch was then aware that he had reached the reported ice region, and so also was the officer who relieved him at 10 p.m. Without implying that those actually on duty were not keeping a good look-out, in view of the night being moonless, there being no wind and perhaps very little swell, and especially in view of the high speed at which the vessel was running, it is not considered that the look-out was sufficient. An extra look-out should, under the circumstances, have been placed at the stemhead, and a sharp look-out should have been kept from both sides of the bridge by an officer.

(c) No directions were given to reduce speed.

11. (a) Were binoculars provided for and used by the look-out men ? (b) Is the use of them necessary or usual in such circumstances ? (c) Had the " Titanic " the means of throwing searchlights around her ? (d) If so, did she make use of them to discover ice ? (e) Should searchlights have been provided and used ?

Answer :

(a) No.

(b) No.

(c) No.

(d) No.

(e) No, but searchlights may at times be of service. The evidence before the Court does not allow of a more precise answer.

12. (a) What other precautions were taken by the " Titanic " in anticipation of meeting ice ? (b) Were they such as are usually adopted by vessels being navigated in waters where ice may be expected to be encountered ?

Answer :

(a) Special orders were given to the men in the crow's nest to keep a sharp look-out for ice, particularly small ice and growlers. The fore scuttle hatch was closed to keep everything dark before the bridge.

(b) Yes, though there is evidence to show that some masters would have placed a look-out at the stemhead of the ship.

13. (a) Was ice seen and reported by anybody on board the " Titanic " before the casualty occurred ? (b) If so, what measures were taken by the officer on watch to avoid it ? (c) Were they proper measures and were they promptly taken ?

Answer :

(a) Yes, immediately before the collision.

(b) The helm was put hard-a-starboard and the engines were stopped and put full speed astern.

(c) Yes.

14. (a) What was the speed of the " Titanic " shortly before and at the moment of the casualty ? (b) Was such speed excessive under the circumstances ?

Answer :

(a) About 22 knots.

(b) Yes.

15. (*a*) What was the nature of the casualty which happened to the " Titanic " at or about 11-45 p.m. on the 14th April last ?   (*b*) In what latitude and longitude did the casualty occur ?

Answer :

(*a*) A collision with an iceberg which pierced the starboard side of the vessel in several places below the water line between the fore peak tank and No. 4 boiler room.

(*b*) In latitude 41° 46' N., longitude 50° 14' W.

16. (*a*) What steps were taken immediately on the happening of the casualty ? (*b*) How long after the casualty was its seriousness realised by those in charge of the vessel ?   (*c*) What steps were then taken ?   (*d*) What endeavours were made to save the lives of those on board, and to prevent the vessel from sinking ?

(*a*) The 12 watertight doors in the engine and boiler rooms were closed from the bridge, some of the boiler fires were drawn, and the bilge pumps abaft No. 6 boiler room were started.

(*b*) About 15–20 minutes.

(*c*) and (*d*) The boats were ordered to be cleared away.   The passengers were roused and orders given to get them on deck, and lifebelts were served out.   Some of the watertight doors, other than those in the boiler and engine rooms, were closed.   Marconigrams were sent out asking for help.   Distress signals (rockets) were fired, and attempts were made to call up by Morse a ship whose lights were seen.   Eighteen of the boats were swung out and lowered, and the remaining two floated off the ship and were subsequently utilized as rafts.

17. Was proper discipline maintained on board after the casualty occurred ?

Answer :

Yes.

18. (*a*) What messages for assistance were sent by the " Titanic " after the casualty and, at what times respectively ?   (*b*) What messages were received by her in response, and at what times respectively ?   (*c*) By what vessels were the messages that were sent by the " Titanic " received, and from what vessels did she receive answers ?   (*d*) What vessels other than the " Titanic " sent or received messages at or shortly after the casualty in connection with such casualty ?   (*e*) What were the vessels that sent or received such messages ?   (*f*) Were any vessels prevented from going to the assistance of the " Titanic " or her boats owing to messages received from the " Titanic " or owing to any erroneous messages being sent or received ? (*g*) In regard to such erroneous messages, from what vessels were they sent and by what vessels were they received and at what times respectively ?

(*a*) (*b*) (*c*) (*d*) and (*e*) are answered together.

(*f*) Several vessels did not go owing to their distance.

(*g*) There were no erroneous messages.

New York Time.	" Titanic " Time (Approx.)		Communications.
10-25 p.m.	12-15 a.m.	...	" La Provence " receives " Titanic " distress signals.
10-25 p.m.	12-15 a.m.	...	" Mount Temple " heard " Titanic " sending C.Q.D. Says require assistance. Gives position. Cannot hear me. Advise my Captain his position 41.46 N. 50.24 W.
10-25 p.m.	12-15 a.m.	...	Cape Race hears " Titanic " giving position on C.Q.D. 41.44 N. 50.24 W.
10-28 p.m.	12-18 a.m.	...	" Ypiranga " hears C.Q.D. from " Titanic." " Titanic " gives C.Q.D. here. Position 41.44 N., 50.24 W. Require assistance (calls about 10 times).
10-35 p.m.	12-25 a.m.	...	C.Q.D. call received from " Titanic " by " Carpathia." " Titanic " said " Come at once. We have struck a berg. It's a C.Q.D. O.M. Position 41.46 N. 50.14 W."
10-35 p.m.	12-25 a.m.	...	Cape Race hears M.G.Y. (" Titanic ") give corrected position 41.46 N. 50.14 W. Calling him, no answer.

E

New York Time.	"Titanic" Time (Approx.)		Communications.
10-36 p.m.	12-26 a.m.	...	M.G.Y. ("Titanic") says C.Q.D. Here corrected position 41.46 N., 50.14 W. Require immediate assistance. We have collision with iceberg. Sinking. Can nothing hear for noise of steam. Sent about 15 to 20 times to "Ypiranga."
10-37 p.m.	12.27 a.m.	...	"Titanic" sends following : "I require assistance immediately. Struck by iceberg in 41.46 N. 50.14 W."
10-40 p.m.	12-30 a.m.	...	"Titanic" gives his position to "Frankfurt," and says, "Tell your Captain to come to our help. We are on the ice."
10-40 p.m.	12-30 a.m.	...	"Caronia" sent C.Q. message to M.B.C. "Baltic" and C.Q.D.: M.G.Y. ("Titanic") struck iceberg, require immediate assistance.
10-40 p.m.			"Mount Temple" hears M.G.Y. ("Titanic") still calling C.Q.D. Our Captain reverses ship. We are about 50 miles off.
10-46 p.m.	12-26 a.m.	...	D.K.F. ("Prinz Friedrich Wilhelm") calls M.G.Y. ("Titanic") and gives position at 12 a.m. 39.47 N. 50.10 W. M.G.Y. ("Titanic") says, "Are you coming to our ? " D.F.T. ("Frankfurt") says, "What is the matter with u ? " M.G.Y. ("Titanic") "We have collision with iceberg. Sinking. Please tell Captain to come." D.F.T. ("Frankfurt") says, "O.K. will tell ? "
10-48 p.m.	12-38 a.m.	...	"Mount Temple" hears "Frankfurt" give M.G.Y. ("Titanic") his position 39.47 N. 52.10 W.
10-55 p.m.	12-45 a.m.	...	"Titanic" calls "Olympic" S.O.S.
11- 0 p.m.	12-50 a.m.	...	"Titanic" calls C.Q.D. and says, "I require immediate assistance. Position 41.46 N. 50.14 W." Received by "Celtic."
11- 3 p.m.	12-53 a.m.	...	"Caronia" to M.B.C. ("Baltic") and S.O.S., "M.G.Y. ("Titanic") C.Q.D. in 41.46 N., 50.14 W. Wants immediate assistance."
11-10 p.m.	1-0 a.m.	...	M.G.Y. gives distress signal. D.D.C. replies. M.G.Y.'s position 41.46 N., 50.14 W. Assistance from D.D.C. not necessary as M.K.C. shortly afterwards answers distress call.
11-10 p.m.	1-0 a.m.	...	"Titanic" replies to "Olympic" and gives his position as 41.46 N., 50.14 W., and says, "We have struck an iceberg."
11-12 p.m.	1-2 a.m.	...	"Titanic" calls "Asian" and said, "Want immediate assistance." "Asian" answered at once and received "Titanic's" position as 41.46 N., 50.14 W., which he immediately takes to the bridge. Captain instructs operator to have "Titanic's" position repeated.
11-12 p.m.	1-2 a.m.	...	"Virginian" calls "Titanic" but gets no response. Cape Race tells "Virginian" to report to his Captain the "Titanic" has struck iceberg and requires immediate assistance.
11-20 p.m.	1-10 a.m.	...	"Titanic" to M.K.C. ("Olympic"), "We are in collision with berg. Sinking Head down. 41.46 N., 50.14 W. Come soon as possible."
11-20 p.m.	1-10 a.m.	...	"Titanic" to M.K.C. ("Olympic"), Captain says, "Get your boats ready. What is your position ? "
11-25 p.m.	1-15 a.m.	...	"Baltic" to "Caronia," "Please tell 'Titanic' we are making towards her."
11-30 p.m.	1-20 a.m.	...	"Virginian" hears M.C.E. (Cape Race) inform M.G.Y. ("Titanic") "that we are going to his assistance. Our position 170 miles N. of 'Titanic.'"

New York Time.	"Titanic" Time (Approx.)		Communications.
11-35 p.m.	1-25 a.m.	...	"Caronia" tells "Titanic," "'Baltic' coming to your assistance."
11-35 p.m.	1-25 a.m.	...	"Olympic" sends position to "Titanic" 4-24 a.m. G.M.T. 40.52 N., 61.18 W. "Are you steering southerly to meet us?" "Titanic" replies, "We are putting the women off in the boats."
11-35 p.m.	1-25 a.m.	...	"Titanic" and "Olympic" work together.
11-37 p.m.	1-27 a.m.	...	M.G.Y. ("Titanic") says, "We are putting the women off in the boats."
11-40 p.m.	1-30 a.m.	...	"Titanic" tells "Olympic," "We are putting passengers off in small boats."
11-45 p.m.	1-35 a.m.	...	"Olympic" asks "Titanic" what weather he had. "Titanic" replies, "Clear and calm."
11-45 p.m.	1-35 a.m.	...	"Baltic" hears "Titanic" say "Engine room getting flooded."
11-45 p.m.	1-35 a.m.	...	"Mount Temple" hears D.F.T. ("Frankfurt") ask "are there any boats around you already?" No reply.
11-47 p.m.	1-37 a.m.	...	"Baltic" tells "Titanic," "We are rushing to you."
11-50 p.m.	1-40 a.m.	...	"Olympic" to "Titanic," "Am lighting up all possible boilers as fast as can."
11-50 p.m.	1-40 a.m.	...	Cape Race says to "Virginian": "Please tell your Captain this: "The 'Olympic' is making all speed for 'Titanic,' but his ('Olympic's') position is 40.32 N., 61.18 W. You are much nearer to 'Titanic.' The 'Titanic' is already putting women off in the boats, and he says the weather there is calm and clear. The 'Olympic' is the only ship we have heard say, "Going to the assistance of the 'Titanic.' The others must be a long way from the 'Titanic.'"
11-55 p.m.	1-45 a.m.	...	Last signals heard from "Titanic" by "Carpathia," "Engine-room full up to boilers."
11-55 p.m.	1-45 a.m.	...	"Mount Temple" hears D.F.T. ("Frankfurt") calling M.G.Y. ("Titanic"). No reply.
11-57 p.m.	1-47 a.m.	...	"Caronia" hears M.G.Y. ("Titanic") though signals unreadable still.
11-58 p.m.	1-48 a.m.	...	"Asian" heard "Titanic" call S.O.S. "Asian" answers "Titanic" but receives no answer.
Midnight.	1-50 a.m.	...	"Caronia" hears "Frankfurt" working to "Titanic." "Frankfurt" according to position 172 miles from M.G.Y. ("Titanic") at time first S.O.S. sent out.
12-5 a.m.	1-55 a.m.	...	Cape Race says to "Virginian" "we have not heard 'Titanic' for about half an hour. His power may be gone."
12-10 a.m.	2-0 a.m.	...	"Virginian" hears "Titanic" calling very faintly, his power being greatly reduced.
12-20 a.m.	2-10 a.m.	...	"Virginian" hears 2 v's signalled faintly in spark similar to "Titanic's" probably adjusting spark.
12-27 a.m.	2-17 a.m.	...	"Virginian" hears "Titanic" call C.Q., but unable to read him. "Titanic's" signals end very abruptly as power suddenly switched off. His spark rather blurred or ragged. Called M.G.Y. ("Titanic") and suggested he should try emergency set, but heard no response.
12-30 a.m.	2-20 a.m.	...	"Olympic," his sigs. strong, asked him if he had heard anything about M.G.Y. ("Titanic") he says, No. Keeping strict watch, but hear nothing more from M.G.Y. ("Titanic"). No reply from him.

E 2

New York Time.	Communications.
12-52 a.m.	This was the official time the "Titanic" foundered in 41.46 N., 50.14 W. as given by the "Carpathia" in message to the "Olympic"; about 2-20 a.m.
1-15 a.m.	"Virginian" exchanges signals "Baltic." He tries send us M.S.G. for M.G.Y. ("Titanic"), but his signals died utterly away.
1-25 a.m.	Mount Temple hears M.P.A. ("Carpathia") send, "If you are there we are firing rockets."
1-35 a.m.	"Baltic" sent 1 M.S.G. to "Virginian" for "Titanic."
1-40 a.m.	M.P.A. ("Carpathia") calling M.G.Y. ("Titanic").
1-58 a.m.	S.B.A. ("Birma") thinks he hears "Titanic" so sends, "Steaming full speed for you. Shall arrive you 6-0 in morning. Hope you are safe. We are only 50 miles now."
2-0 a.m.	M.P.A. ("Carpathia") calling M.G.Y. ("Titanic).
2-0 a.m.	Have not heard "Titanic" since 11-50 p.m. Received from "Ypiranga."
2-28 a.m.	"La Provence" to "Celtic," "Nobody has heard the "Titanic" for about 2 hours."
3-24 a.m.	S.B.A. ("Birma") says we are 30 miles S.W. off "Titanic."
3-35 a.m.	"Celtic" sends message to "Caronia" for the "Titanic." "Caronia" after trying for two hours to get through to the "Titanic" tells the "Celtic" impossible to clear his message to "Titanic." "Celtic" then cancels message.
3-45 a.m.	"Californian" exchanges signals with M.L.Q. (Mount Temple). He gave position of "Titanic."
4-10 a.m.	"Californian" receives M.S.G. from M.G.N ("Virginian").
5-5 a.m.	"Baltic" signals M.P.A. ("Carpathia").
5-40 a.m.	"Parisian" hears weak signals from M.P.A. ("Carpathia") or some station saying "Titanic" struck iceberg. "Carpathia" has passengers from lifeboats.
5-40 a.m.	"Olympic Tr Asian," with German oil tank in tow for "Halifax" asked what news of M.G.Y. ("Titanic"). Sends service later saying heard M.G.Y. ("Titanic") v. faint wkg. C. Race up to 10.0 p.m., local time. Finished calling S.O.S. midnight.
6-5 a.m.	"Parisian" exchanges TRs "Virginian" O.K. nil. Informed Captain Haines what I heard passing between ships regarding "Titanic," and he decided not to return as M.P.A. ("Carpathia") was there, and "Californian" was 50 miles astern of us but requested me to stand by in case required.
6-45 a.m.	Mount Temple hears M.P.A. ("Carpathia") report rescued 20 boat loads.
7-7 a.m.	"Baltic" sends following to "Carpathia": "Can I be of any assistance to you as regards taking some of the passengers from you? Will be in position about 4-30. Let me know if you alter your position."
7-10 a.m.	"Baltic" in communication with M.P.A. ("Carpathia"). Exchanged traffic re passengers, and get instructions to proceed to Liverpool.
7-15 a.m.	"Baltic" turns round for Liverpool, having steamed 134 miles W. towards "Titanic."
7-40 a.m.	Mount Temple hears M.P.A. ("Carpathia") call C.Q. and say, no need to std. bi him. Advise my Captain, who has been cruising round the icefield with no result. Ship reversed.
7-45 a.m.	"Olympic" sent M.S.G. to Owners, New York via Sable Island, saying, "Have not communicated with 'Titanic' since midnight."
7-55 a.m.	"Carpathia" replies to "Baltic," "Am proceeding to Halifax or New York full speed. You had better proceed to Liverpool. Have about 800 passengers on board."
8-0 a.m.	"Carpathia" to "Virginian": "We are leaving here with all on board about 800 passengers. Please return to your Northern course."

19. (a) Was the apparatus for lowering the boats on the "Titanic" at the time of the casualty in good working order? (b) Were the boats swung out, filled, lowered, or otherwise put into the water and got away under proper superintendence? (c) Were the boats sent away in seaworthy condition and properly manned, equipped and provisioned? (d) Did the boats, whether those under davits or otherwise, prove to be efficient and serviceable for the purpose of saving life?

Answer:

(a) Yes.

(b) Yes.

(c) The fourteen lifeboats, two emergency boats, and C and D collapsible boats were sent away in a seaworthy condition, but some of them were possibly undermanned. The evidence on this point was unsatisfactory. The total number of crew taken on board the "Carpathia" exceeded the number which would be required for for manning the boats. The collapsible boats A and B appear to have floated off the ship at the time she foundered. The necessary equipment and provisions for the boats were carried in the ship, but some of the boats, nevertheless, left without having their full equipment in them.

(d) Yes.

20. (a) What was the number of (a) passengers, (b) crew taken away in each boat on leaving the vessel? (b) How was this number made up, having regard to:—

1. Sex.
2. Class.
3. Rating.

(c) How many were children and how many adults? (d) Did each boat carry its full load and, if not, why not?

Answer:

(a) (b) (c) It is impossible exactly to say how many persons were carried in each boat or what was their sex, class and rating, as the totals given in evidence do not correspond with the numbers taken on board the "Carpathia."

The boats eventually contained in all 712 persons made up as shown in the answer to Question 21.

(d) No.

At least 8 boats did not carry their full loads for the following reasons:—

1. Many people did not realise the danger or care to leave the ship at first.
2. Some boats were ordered to be lowered with an idea of their coming round to the gangway doors to complete loading.
3. The officers were not certain of the strength and capacity of the boats in all cases (and see p. 39).

21. (a) How many persons on board the "Titanic" at the time of the casualty were ultimately rescued and by what means? (b) How many lost their lives prior to the arrival of the ss. "Carpathia" in New York? (c) What was the number of passengers, distinguishing between men and women and adults and children of the 1st, 2nd, and 3rd classes respectively who were saved? (d) What was the number of the crew, discriminating their ratings and sex, that were saved? (e) What is the proportion which each of these numbers bears to the corresponding total number on board immediately before the casualty? (f) What reason is there for the disproportion, if any?

Answer:

(a) 712, rescued by "Carpathia" from the boats.

(b) One.

(c) (d) and (e) are answered together.

The following is a list of the saved :—

1st Class.

Adult Males	...	...	57	out of 175, or 32.57 per cent.
Adult Females	...	...	140	out of 144, or 97.22 per cent.
Male children	...	...	5	All saved.
Female children	...	...	1	All saved.
			203	out of 325 or 62.46 per cent.

2nd Class.

Adult Males	...	...	14	out of 168, or 8.33 per cent.
Adult Females	...	...	80	out of 93, or 86.02 per cent.
Male children	...	...	11	All saved.
Female children	...	...	13	All saved.
			118	out of 285, or 41.40 per cent.

3rd Class.

Adult Males	...	...	75	out of 462, or 16.23 per cent.
Adult Females	...	...	76	out of 165, or 46.06 per cent.
Male children	...	...	13	out of 48, or 27.08 per cent.
Female children	...	...	14	out of 31, or 45.16 per cent.
			178	out of 706, or 25.21 per cent.
Total Passengers	...	...	499	out of 1,316, or 37.94 per cent.

Crew saved.

Deck Department ...	...	43	out of 66, or 65.15 per cent.
Engine Room Department		72	out of 325, or 22.15 per cent.
Victualling Department	...	97	out of 494, or 19.63 per cent.
Including Women ...	...	20	out of 23, or 86.95 per cent.
		212	out of 885, or 23.95 per cent.
Total on board saved	...	711	out of 2,201, or 32.30 per cent.

(f) The disproportion between the numbers of the passengers saved in the first, second, and third classes is due to various causes, among which the difference in the position of their quarters and the fact that many of the third class passengers were foreigners, are perhaps the most important. Of the Irish emigrants in the third class a large proportion was saved. The disproportion was certainly not due to any discrimination by the officers or crew in assisting the passengers to the boats. The disproportion between the numbers of the passengers and crew saved is due to the fact that the crew, for the most part, all attended to their duties to the last, and until all the boats were gone.

22.   What happened to the vessel from the happening of the casualty until she foundered ?

Answer :

A detailed description has already been given (see pages 32-34.)

23.   Where and at what time did the " Titanic " founder ?

Answer :

2-20 a.m. (ship's time) 15th April.
Latitude 41° 46' N., longitude 50° 14' W.

24. (*a*) What was the cause of the loss of the " Titanic," and of the loss of life which thereby ensued or occurred ? (*b*) What vessels had the opportunity of rendering assistance to the " Titanic " and, if any, how was it that assistance did not reach the " Titanic " before the ss. " Carpathia " arrived ? (*c*) Was the construction of the vessel and its arrangements such as to make it difficult for any class of passenger or any portion of the crew to take full advantage of any of the existing provisions for safety ?

Answer :

(*a*) Collision with an iceberg and the subsequent foundering of the ship.

(*b*) The " Californian." She could have reached the " Titanic " if she had made the attempt when she saw the first rocket. She made no attempt.

(*c*) No.

25. When the " Titanic " left Queenstown on or about April 11th last was she properly constructed, and adequately equipped as a passenger steamer and emigrant ship for the Atlantic service ?

Answer :

Yes.

26. The Court is invited to report upon the Rules and Regulations made under the Merchant Shipping Acts, 1894–1906, and the administration of those Acts and of such Rules and Regulations, so far as the consideration thereof is material to this casualty, and to make any recommendations or suggestions that it may think fit, having regard to the circumstances of the casualty, with a view to promoting the safety of vessels and persons at sea.

Answer :

An account of the Board of Trade's Administration has already been given and certain recommendations are subsequently made.

RECOMMENDATIONS.

The following Recommendations are made. They refer to foreign-going Passenger and Emigrant Steamships.

Water-tight Sub-division.

1. That the newly appointed Bulkhead Committee should enquire and report, among other matters, on the desirability aud practicability of providing ships with (a) a double skin carried up above the waterline: or, as an alternative, with (b) a longitudinal, vertical, watertight bulkhead on each side of the ship, extending as far forward and aft as convenient: or (c) with a combination of (a) and (b). Any one of the three (a), (b) and (c) to be in addition to watertight transverse bulkheads.

2. That the Committee should also enquire and report as to the desirability and practicability of fitting ships with (a) a deck or decks at a convenient distance or distances above the waterline which shall be watertight throughout a part or the whole of the ship's length: and should in this connection report upon (b) the means by which the necessary openings in such deck or decks should be made watertight, whether by watertight doors or watertight trunks or by any other and what means.

3. That the Committee should consider and report generally on the practicability of increasing the protection given by sub-division; the object being to secure that the ship shall remain afloat with the greatest practicable proportion of her length in free communication with the sea.

4. That when the Committee has reported upon the matters before mentioned, the Board of Trade should take the report into their consideration and to the extent to which they approve of it should seek Statutory powers to enforce it in all newly built ships, but with a discretion to relax the requirements in special cases where it may seem right to them to do so.

5. That the Board of Trade should be empowered by the Legislature to require the production of the designs and specifications of all ships in their early stages of construction and to direct such amendments of the same as may be thought necessary and practicable for the safety of life at sea in ships. (This should apply to all passenger carrying ships.)

Lifeboats and Rafts.

6. That the provision of life boat and raft accommodation on board such ships should be based on the number of persons intended to be carried in the ship and not upon tonnage.

7. That the question of such accommodation should be treated independently of the question of the sub-division of the ship into watertight compartments. (This involves the abolition of Rule 12 of the Life Saving Appliances Rules of 1902.)

8. That the accommodation should be sufficient for all persons on board, with, however, the qualification that in special cases where, in the opinion of the Board of Trade, such provision is impracticable, the requirements may be modified as the Board may think right. (In order to give effect to this recommendation changes may be necessary in the sizes and types of boats to be carried and in the method of stowing and floating them. It may also be necessary to set apart one or more of the boat decks exclusively for carrying boats and drilling the crew, and to consider the distribution of decks in relation to the passengers' quarters. These, however, are matters of detail to be settled with reference to the particular circumstance affecting the ship).

9. That all boats should be fitted with a protective, continuous fender, to lessen the risk of damage when being lowered in a seaway.

10. That the Board of Trade should be empowered to direct that one or more of the boats be fitted with some form of mechanical propulsion.

11. That there should be a Board of Trade regulation requiring all boat equipment (under sections 5 and 6, page 15 of the Rules, dated February, 1902, made by the Board of Trade under section 427 Merchant Shipping Act, 1894) to be in the boats as soon as the ship leaves harbour. The sections quoted above should be amended so as to provide also that all boats and rafts should carry lamps and pyrotechnic lights for purposes of signalling. All boats should be provided with compasses and provisions, and should be very distinctly marked in such a way as to indicate plainly the number of adult persons each boat can carry when being lowered.

12. That the Board of Trade inspection of boats and life-saving appliances should be of a more searching character than hitherto.

Manning the Boats and Boat Drills.

13. That in cases where the deck hands are not sufficient to man the boats enough other members of the crew should be men trained in boat work to make up the deficiency. These men should be required to pass a test in boat work.

14. That in view of the necessity of having on board men trained in boat work, steps should be taken to encourage the training of boys for the Merchant Service.

15. That the operation of Section 115 and Section 134 (a) of the Merchant Shipping Act, 1894, should be examined, with a view to amending the same so as to secure greater continuity of service than hitherto.

16. That the men who are to man the boats should have more frequent drills than hitherto. That in all ships a boat drill, a fire-drill and a watertight door drill should be held as soon as possible after leaving the original port of departure and at convenient intervals of not less than once a week during the voyage. Such drills to be recorded in the official log.

17. That the Board of Trade should be satisfied in each case before the ship leaves port that a scheme has been devised and communicated to each officer of the ship for securing an efficient working of the boats.

General.

18. That every man taking a look-out in such ships should undergo a sight test at reasonable intervals.

19. That in all such ships a police system should be organised so as to secure obedience to orders, and proper control and guidance of all on board in times of emergency.

20. That in all such ships there should be an installation of wireless telegraphy, and that such installation should be worked with a sufficient number of trained operators to secure a continuous service by night and day. In this connection regard should be had to the resolutions of the International Conference on Wireless Telegraphy recently held under the presidency of Sir H. Babington Smith. That where practicable a silent chamber for " receiving " messages should form part of the installation.

21. That instruction should be given in all Steamship Companies' Regulations that when ice is reported in or near the track the ship should proceed in the dark hours at a moderate speed or alter her course so as to go well clear of the danger zone.

22. That the attention of Masters of vessels should be drawn by the Board of Trade to the effect that under the Maritime Conventions Act, 1911, it is a misdemeanour not to go to the relief of a vessel in distress when possible to do so.

F

23.   That the same protection as to the safety of life in the event of casualty which is afforded to emigrant ships by means of supervision and inspection should be extended to all foreign-going passenger ships.

24.   That (unless already done) steps should be taken to call an International Conference to consider and as far as possible to agree upon a common line of conduct in respect of (*a*) the subdivision of ships; (*b*) the provision and working of life-saving appliances; (*c*) the installation of wireless telegraphy and the method of working the same, (*d*) the reduction of speed or the alteration of course in the vicinity of ice, and (*e*) the use of searchlights.

MERSEY,

Wreck Commissioner.

We concur

ARTHUR GOUGH-CALTHORPE,

A. W. CLARKE,

F. C. A. LYON,   *Assessors.*

J. H. BILES,

EDWARD C. CHASTON.

30*th July,* 1912.

Almas

Yeti

Mokele-Mbembe

Kongamato

PAUL ROBERT WALKER

Illustrated by William Noonan

Harcourt Brace & Company

SAN DIEGO   NEW YORK   LONDON

Requests for permission to make copies of any part of the work should
be mailed to: Permissions Department, Harcourt Brace & Company,
6277 Sea Harbor Drive, Orlando, Florida 32887-6777.

The author is indebted to the International Society of Cryptozoology,
P. O. Box 43070, Tucson, Arizona, 85733. Membership in the Society is
open to anyone interested in the scientific study of unknown animals.

Library of Congress Cataloging-in-Publication Data
Walker, Paul Robert.
Bigfoot and other legendary creatures/by Paul Robert Walker;
illustrated by William Noonan.—1st ed.
p. cm.
Summary: Explores the myths and scientific inquiries surrounding
repeated sightings of such legendary creatures as the
Loch Ness monster, Bigfoot, and the Yeti.
ISBN 0-15-207147-4
ISBN 0-15-201551-5 (pb)
1. Monsters—Juvenile literature. [1. Monsters.] I. Noonan, William,
1923–   , ill. II. Title.
QL89.W34   1992
001.9'44—dc20   90-45856

Designed by Michael Farmer

C E G F D
A C E F D B (pb)

Printed in Singapore

To Devin, the legendary creature in our house.
—P. R.W.

To Shon, whose future is bright.
—W. N.

Contents

Introduction

THIS IS A BOOK ABOUT MONSTERS. Not movie monsters or fantasy monsters or monsters that live under your bed. No, the monsters in this book are large, living, breathing creatures that share our world without our knowledge. Impossible, you say? After all, we know everything, don't we? Consider the story of the okapi.

In 1860 the British journalist H. M. Stanley described how the Pygmies who lived in the tropical rain forests of the Congo (now Zaire) captured a wild donkey called an *atti*. According to zoologists, scientists who study living animals, there were no donkeys in the Congo. The only animal that might be mistaken for a donkey was the zebra, but zebras didn't live in the rain forests.

Almost forty years later, in 1899, a British official named Sir Harry Johnston asked a group of Pygmies about the atti. They told him that it was actually called the okapi and that it was a mule with stripes like a zebra. Sir Harry searched for more information about this strange creature, but the more he found out, the stranger the creature became. It seemed to be a small horse with hooves like an antelope, ears like a donkey, and stripes like a zebra.

Knowing of Sir Harry's interest in the okapi, another colonial official sent him a skin and two skulls of the mysterious animal. After studying this evidence, zoologists realized that the okapi was not a horse or an antelope or a donkey or a zebra. It was actually a short-necked relative of the giraffe! In fact, it was a type of giraffe that existed long before the modern-day giraffe. Today, the okapi is no longer a mystery. You can probably see one at your local zoo.

Now, the okapi is hardly a monster. But it *is* a large, unusual creature that existed for thousands of years without the knowledge of the scientific world. Of course the Pygmies knew all about it, but most scientists don't believe reports from native people. Scientists want cold, hard facts. Fortunately, there are a few open-minded researchers like Sir Harry Johnston who are willing to listen to native reports. And it is these reports that usually lead to the great discoveries.

The okapi is not the only large, unknown animal that was discovered in the last hundred years. Others include the mountain gorilla (1901), the Komodo dragon (1912), and the pygmy chimpanzee (1929). Megamouth, a fifteen-foot shark that represents a completely new species, was discovered in 1976. The most amazing discovery, however, was the coelacanth, a six-foot fish that was caught off the coast of South Africa in 1938. What's so amazing about that? Well, scientists believed that the coelacanth became extinct over 65 million years ago!

In 1982 the okapi was chosen as the symbol of the International Society of Cryptozoology, a scientific organization dedicated to the investigation of unusual animals that are not yet accepted by the scientific world. "Cryptozoology," the study of hidden animals, is a word created by zoologist Dr. Bernard Heuvelmans. According to Dr. Heuvelmans, there may be at least 138 different kinds of large, unknown animals in the world today.

Seven of these mysterious creatures are described in this book. They are among the biggest, strangest, and scariest of the unknown animals—ranging from huge ape-men to giant water beasts to living dinosaurs. Each of these "monsters" has been described by native people and investigated by serious researchers.

The search for unknown animals requires scientific knowledge and methods. But it also requires an open mind and a vivid imagination. This book is a combination of science and imagination. The descriptions and details in each story are based on reports from people who claim to have seen these creatures and on the opinions of scientists and other experts. The characters and events in the stories are the products of imagination. At the end of each story, there is a nonfiction section that tells about the research and scientific ideas concerning the creature.

Perhaps someday you will combine your imagination and your scientific knowledge and find an okapi of your own. Or a Bigfoot. Or a Loch Ness Monster. Or ???

—P.R.W.

THE BIGFOOT

THE FORESTS of northern California are dense and dark. Giant redwood trees tower above the forest floor, blocking the light of the sun. Between the tall trees, gnarled manzanita bushes grow like blood-red demons. The land is mountainous and roads are few. It is the perfect place for a man to disappear—a man or a beast.

One day a few years ago, a boy and his father ventured into this wilderness to hunt for deer. The boy, whose name was Jack, had just turned thirteen, and he carried his birthday present in a leather case strapped to his backpack. It was a brand-new rifle.

As the afternoon grew late, Jack and his father set up their camp in a clearing near a small creek. They built a fire and cooked their dinner. Then they sat and watched the crackling flames.

"It sure is quiet here," said Jack.

"Don't let it fool you, son. These mountains are full of creatures. Deer. Elk. Grizzlies . . ."

"I want a big buck with antlers this wide." Jack stretched his arms out to the sides as far as they could go.

"You just might get one. You've got the rifle for it. Of course you better look behind you. This is Bigfoot country."

"Bigfoot?"

His father smiled and threw another log onto the fire. For a moment, the flames disappeared beneath the wood; then the red tongues of fire reappeared, consuming the fresh fuel.

"That's right, son. From what I've heard, a grizzly's got nothing on Bigfoot. He's as tall as the trees and as wide as the mountains. The Indians used to say he was a devil who stole their animals and ate their children whole. Some folks say he's a wild man or a big ape that walks like a man. Of course other folks say he's just imagination."

"What do you say?"

Jack's father yawned and stretched. "I say it's time to go to bed. All this fresh air makes me sleepy."

"Can I stay up for a while?"

"Just for a while. Those big bucks get up early."

As his father crawled into the tent, Jack wrapped his sleeping bag around his shoulders and inched closer to the fire. The flames created a warm circle of light that disappeared into the shadows of the clearing. Beyond the clearing loomed the black forest.

Jack had a big day ahead of him, but he was too excited to turn in. He stared into the fire, imagining big bucks and other stranger creatures that walked the woods. As he daydreamed, his eyes grew heavier and heavier. Soon he was asleep.

A rustling of leaves . . . the sound of heavy footsteps. Jack opened his eyes. The fire had burned down; it was the middle of the night.

The steps grew nearer, and there was a horrible smell—worse than a skunk, worse than anything he had ever smelled before. His heart pounded in his chest. Jack glanced toward the tent where his father was sleeping.

A huge figure stood in the light of the dying flames . . .

The wooden stock of his brand-new rifle was only a few feet away, but he was afraid to move. He was afraid to breathe.

He turned back toward the fire. A huge figure stood in the light of the dying flames. Its body was covered with long hair. Its chest was broad, and its arms hung to its knees. Its face . . .

Jack gurgled in horror. He was dreaming—he had to be. It wasn't real. It had the face of an ape, with bony brow, flat nose, huge jaw, and deep black eyes. But it wasn't like any ape he had seen in a zoo. It was eight feet tall, and it stood like a man. It was Bigfoot.

Jack screamed without sound. He was too frightened for sound. Slowly, the huge creature walked around the fire. It stood directly over the boy, as tall and as massive as the giant redwoods. Then it reached down and scooped Jack up with its huge hands. Turning away from the fire, it carried the boy toward the dark woods.

"Dad!" Jack screamed. "Daaaaaad!" This time there was sound.

His father scrambled out of the tent, but all he found was a deserted fire. Jack was gone.

Deep into the woods, the creature carried the boy. Jack tried to scream, but the Bigfoot pressed his face against its broad, muscular chest. Shaggy, rank-smelling hair filled Jack's mouth. He gagged and tried to cough it out, nauseated by the sickening odor of the beast.

After what seemed like hours, the giant ape set the boy gently on the ground. Jack could hear another animal shuffling around him in the darkness. Furry hands touched his face and stroked his body. Shaking with fear and cold, Jack slumped onto the forest floor and whimpered quietly to himself.

Later, when the gray light of dawn filtered through the trees, Jack lifted his head from the ground and gazed at the beasts. A seven-foot female Bigfoot stood beside the eight-foot giant. She wasn't as heavy or as muscular as

the male Bigfoot, but she was monstrous by human standards. The creatures stared at Jack as if they were waiting for him to do something. Then, very slowly, the female Bigfoot walked toward him.

"Please!" Jack begged. "Please don't hurt me!"

The Bigfoot stopped less than a yard away. Jack breathed her foul stench and looked into the black depths of her eyes. There was something very human in her gaze. Something sad, regretful . . . almost longing.

"You . . . you won't hurt me, will you?"

The Bigfoot raised her right hand and reached toward Jack's face with her long, apelike arm. Jack shrank from her approach; a low moan escaped his lips. He couldn't move. He was paralyzed by fear—and fascination.

Lightly, almost tenderly, she touched his cheek and rubbed her rough palm along the line of his jaw. She took another step forward and wrapped her long, hairy arms around him. Pulling the boy gently against her body, she cradled him as if he were a lost child. Jack felt warm and safe. For the first time since the eight-foot giant had carried him away from the fire, he was not afraid.

A shot rang out in the forest. Releasing the boy, the female Bigfoot howled in terror. "*Aaagooooummm!*" Then she turned and disappeared into the trees, followed by her mate.

Jack was alone.

"Jaaaaaaack! Jaaaaaaack!"

"Dad! Over here!"

Jack's father broke through the trees. He set his rifle against a log and held his son close. "Are you all right?" he asked. "You smell horrible!"

"It was Bigfoot!"

"Bigfoot? What are you talking about?"

As Jack told the story, his father eyed him in disbelief. "That's just a legend, son. I didn't expect you to take it seriously."

8

"It was real, Dad. I promise. Look at the tracks."

His father knelt down to examine the forest floor. There were a few broken twigs but no footprints. The ground was too hard. "I don't know, son. Maybe you had a bad dream and walked in your sleep."

"It wasn't a dream."

"C'mon, let's have some breakfast."

"Dad?"

"Yes?"

"That shot—did you hit anything?"

His father shook his head. "I was just shooting in the air."

"Good. . . . Is it okay if I don't use my rifle? I mean, can I wait until tomorrow? I just don't feel like hunting today."

Jack's father eyed him strangely. Then he smiled and shrugged. "It's your gun. Use it when you're ready."

On the way back to camp, Jack looked for signs of the Bigfoot, but there was nothing. How could two huge creatures vanish without a trace? Maybe his father was right. Maybe it really was a dream. But dreams don't smell. Do they?

When they got to their campsite, Jack examined the soft, damp ground along the creek. Huge footprints led from the edge of the forest, along the creek, and curved toward the cold remains of the fire. There was no doubt about it. He had been kidnapped by Bigfoot.

Stories of huge, hairy wild men have been told by the Indians of the Pacific Northwest for hundreds of years. The Salish Indians of British Columbia called the creature Sasquatch, which means "wild man of the woods." This name is still used in Canada today. The Huppa Indians of northern California called the creature Oh-Ma, which means "Bigfoot."

Bigfoot tracks have been found throughout the rugged mountains of northern California, Oregon, Washington, and British Columbia. These tracks are similar to barefoot human tracks, but larger, farther apart, and pressed more deeply into the ground. Most of the prints are around fourteen to eighteen inches long and five to seven inches wide. A creature with a foot of this size would be over seven feet eight inches tall and might weigh up to 800 pounds. These footprints have been found in rugged, remote areas, where it would be difficult to use a "footprint machine" to create a hoax. Some prints demonstrate special characteristics, such as deformities or dermal ridges (similar to fingerprints) that would be almost impossible to fake.

More than 2,000 people have reported seeing the Bigfoot. Most reports describe a giant, apelike creature walking on two feet like a human being. (All known apes and monkeys walk on four feet.) By combining the descriptions of many eye-witnesses, researchers have created a picture of a "typical" Bigfoot. This descrip-

tion is the basis for the two Bigfoots in this story. A few reports have described kidnapping or other aggressive behavior by the Bigfoots; however, the vast majority of reports indicate a shy creature who poses no threat to human beings.

In 1967 a man named Roger Patterson shot a short color film that appears to show a female Bigfoot walking through a clearing and into the woods. She's between six and one-half and seven feet tall, weighs about 350 pounds, and walks upright like a human being, with her arms swinging to the sides. Patterson's film has been analyzed by many experts, but no one has been able to prove whether it is real or a hoax. However, experts at Disney Studios said it would be impossible to fake such a film using a man in a costume.

Similar mysterious apelike creatures have been reported in many other areas of the world. The most famous is the Yeti, or Abominable Snowman, said to live in the Himalaya Mountains of Asia (see page 12). The Yeti seems to be somewhat smaller than the Bigfoot and sometimes travels on four feet, while the Bigfoot is always reported on two feet. Chinese scientists are investigating a large, two-footed apelike creature called the Wildman, said to live in the Shen Nong Jia Mountains of central China. Some researchers believe that the Bigfoot, the Wildman, and perhaps the Yeti, may be the descendants—or living specimens—of a prehistoric ape called Gigantopithecus.

THE YETI

ANCHE LOOKED OUT over her flock of sheep, grazing contentedly in the alpine meadow. High above the meadow, the snowy peak of Mount Everest stretched against the clear blue sky. *The top of the world*, thought Kanche. It was more than twenty miles away, but the craggy white peak looked so huge and majestic that she almost thought she could touch it.

Out of the corner of her eye, Kanche caught a flicker of movement. One of her sheep had strayed away from the flock. It was heading toward the edge of the meadow, where the rolling ground dropped off sharply into the deep valley of the Dudh Kosi River. In a single motion, Kanche ran toward the sheep, picked up a rock, and hurled it in the path of the animal. Bleating loudly, the sheep turned away and returned to the rest of the flock.

Kanche smiled proudly. Like most Sherpa children, she had been tending her family's livestock since she was very young. Her arm was strong and her aim was true. Even her brother, Tenzing, could throw no better than that. Kanche could see Tenzing at the far end of the meadow, leaning casually against a boulder as the yaks and zums grazed among the juniper

bushes. Next year he would go to high school in another village. Then Kanche would watch all the animals herself.

The top of the world was bathed in brilliant sunshine, but cold shadows crept across the meadow, inching up the steep, rocky slope that rose toward the mountains. Although the meadow was green with grass, the slope was covered with eternal snow. Kanche gazed at the cold, white blanket falling gradually under the spell of darkness. Something moved in the snow, near the line between the shadows and the sunlight. Kanche rubbed her eyes and looked again. This time there was nothing. At least nothing she could see. But she felt as if something—or someone—were watching.

"Kanche! Time to go!" Tenzing broke her concentration. He was already leading the yaks and zums back toward the village.

"Wait for me!" cried Kanche. Quickly, she began to herd her sheep across the meadow. That Tenzing! He was always in such a hurry. Kanche pushed her sheep as quickly as she could. "Loh! Loh! Let's go!" She prodded them with her stick and threw rocks in the path of strays, but the sheep were slow and stupid. By the time she had them all out of the meadow and onto the road to the village, Tenzing was out of sight.

Kanche glanced back toward the rocky slope. It was covered in shadow now, but she still felt as if she were being watched. She stared through the gray twilight for signs of movement, but there was nothing. "Loh! Loh!" she called to the sheep. "Let's go!"

As she herded the animals toward the village, the darkness grew deeper and deeper. Soon even the top of the world was lost in the night. There was no moon. The only light was the soft glow of the stars.

"*Bahhhhh! Bahhhhh!*" The stillness was broken by the pitiful bleating of a sheep. Peering through the darkness, Kanche saw a huge creature on the other side of the flock. It stood upright like a man, but it was bigger and

But it wasn't a monkey. And it wasn't a man. It was the Yeti . . .

hairier than a man, with the long arms and ugly face of a monkey. Kanche watched frozen in horror as it bent over one of her sheep. It lifted the heavy animal as if it were a newborn lamb and slung it over its broad shoulders.

Kanche's horror turned to anger—it was stealing her sheep! She picked up a rock and hurled it toward the beast, hitting it squarely between the eyes.

"*Owooooooh!*" it howled in a high, hideous voice. For a moment it stared at Kanche, its red eyes glowing in the black gloom. Then it disappeared into the night, carrying the sheep.

"*Bahhhhh! Bahhhhh! Bahhhhh!*" The flock was fearful and restless. Kanche stood shaking, her teeth chattering. The night was growing cold, but it wasn't the cold that made Kanche tremble. It was the monkey-man.

"Loh! Loh!" she called. "Let's go!" Kanche tried to sound brave for the sake of the sheep. They were dumb animals; maybe they would believe her.

When Kanche reached the village, she herded the flock into the dark space beneath her family's house. The yaks and zums were already bedded down for the night. After the sheep were settled, she climbed the stairs to the living quarters. There was one large room, where her family lived, cooked, and slept. Her mother was preparing a meal of potatoes in the earthen stove. Her father, grandfather, and brother sat around the Tibetan brazier, warming themselves at the fire.

"You're late," said Tenzing.

"What's wrong, child?" asked her mother, glancing up from the cooking pot. "You look like you saw a demon!"

"I lost a sheep," said Kanche.

"What?" cried her father. "How could you lose a sheep?"

"It *was* a demon," said Kanche. "It had red eyes and the face of a monkey."

"What are you talking about?" asked her father.

"Let the girl speak," said her grandfather. "Here, child, sit by the fire."

Kanche sat beside her grandfather and told her story from the beginning, when she first saw something moving in the shadows on the snow. When she was finished, her father rose angrily and reached for the shiny rifle he had brought from Kathmandu. "A bear," he said. "I think I will teach it a lesson."

"Put the rifle away," said Kanche's grandfather. "The Sherpas do not need guns."

"What are you talking about, old man? That bear killed my sheep."

"It is not a bear. Kanche, bring me the *chang*."

Kanche crossed the great room and picked up the large jar of beerlike *chang*.

"*Chang!*" cried Kanche's father. "How is *chang* going to stop a bear?"

Kanche's grandfather rose slowly from his seat by the fire. "My son," he said, "I have told you it is not a bear. It is a Yeti. The Snowman. Come, Kanche, we have work to do."

Kanche and her grandfather walked back along the road toward the meadow. It was completely black now, and the wind howled down from the top of the world. The jar of *chang* was cold and heavy in Kanche's hands. But she was not afraid of the cold. She was afraid of the Snowman.

"Do you really think it is a Yeti?" she whispered.

Her grandfather walked briskly, shining the beam of a small flashlight on the ground ahead of them. "Of course it is a Yeti, child. I have lived in these mountains for a very long time, and I have never known a bear to have the face of a monkey or to carry a sheep and walk like a man."

"Do you think it's watching us?" asked Kanche.

The old man shrugged his shoulders. "It is possible. But we are in no danger. He has his sheep."

"But if he is full of sheep, how will he drink the *chang?*"

The old man smiled slightly, keeping his eyes on the road ahead. "He will drink. I have never known a Yeti who refused *chang*."

When they reached the place in the road where the Yeti had attacked Kanche's sheep, Kanche opened the jar of *chang* and set it on a flat rock. "Good," said her grandfather, "now we will go home and sleep."

"But what if he comes?" asked Kanche.

Her grandfather laughed and pointed the beam of the flashlight toward the village. "If he comes, he will drink. If he drinks, he will drink too much. If he drinks too much, he will sleep. If he sleeps, we will find him in the morning."

Early the next morning, before the sun rose above the mountains, Kanche and her grandfather returned to the place where they had left the *chang*. The jar was empty, and a huge shape lay beside it. The beast was over six feet tall and covered with coarse gray hair. It had the face and long, dangling arms of a monkey. But it wasn't a monkey. And it wasn't a man. It was the Yeti.

"Look, Grandfather!" cried Kanche. "There, in his forehead. You can see where I hit him with the stone."

"Your aim was true," said the old man. "I think this Yeti has a headache."

Kanche's grandfather knelt down over the sleeping beast and began to wrap a thick cord around its arms and chest. Then he wrapped another cord around its ankles. Just as he finished, the beast began to stir. "Stand back, child!" her grandfather cried. "On the other side of the road."

Kanche did as she was told. Her heart beat quickly as she watched the creature sit up slowly and look at its surroundings. It seemed confused and afraid. After a few moments it tried to stand up. When it felt the ropes, it howled like a wild man. "*Owoooooooh! Owoooooooh!*" The creature looked back and forth between Kanche and her grandfather, staring at them with

red, burning eyes. *"Owooooooh!"* With one great effort, it strained against the ropes and ripped them apart.

The Yeti towered above Kanche's grandfather. Kanche grabbed a rock and took careful aim at the beast. When the Yeti saw the rock in Kanche's hand, it howled in terror and ran toward the meadow. It fled like a wild man across the rolling ground and scrambled up the rocky slope, disappearing into the eternal snow.

Kanche's grandfather stood beside the empty jar of *chang*, a broken piece of rope in his bony hands, gazing sadly toward the slope. "They will never believe us," he said.

Kanche dropped the rock. Then she crossed the road and put her arms around the old man. "That's all right, Grandfather. We know the truth."

"Yes"—he nodded—"and so does that Yeti." Slowly his old wrinkled face broke into a broad grin. "I don't think we'll be losing any more sheep."

Stories of mysterious wild men have been told by the people of the Himalayas for hundreds of years—they are especially common among the Sherpas, a tribe of hardy, cheerful people who live beneath Mount Everest in Nepal. Many ideas in this story, including the Yeti's fondness for chang, are based on Sherpa folktales.

The word Yeti is an English version of yeh-teh, a Nepalese word that means "snowman." The term Abominable Snowman comes from the Tibetan name for the creature, Metoh-Kangmi, which means "filthy or disgusting snowman."

Since the early nineteenth century, British diplomats, military officers, and explorers have reported seeing strange creatures or footprints in the Himalayas. However, it was not until 1951 that the Yeti became famous in the Western world. A British mountain climber named Eric Shipton discovered a strange set of footprints on the Menlung Glacier at an elevation of 18,000 feet. On the same day, he discovered another print that was thirteen inches long and eight inches wide with clearly defined toes. Shipton's photographs of the footprints were published throughout the world.

During the last forty years, scientific and mountaineering expeditions have continued to encounter strange footprints in the snows of the Himalayas. In 1970, a British mountain climber named Don Whillans photographed supposed Yeti tracks at an elevation of 13,000 feet. That night—in bright moonlight—Whillans observed an apelike creature running on four legs across a hillside. In 1986, German mountaineer Reinhold Messner claimed to see a Yeti at a range of thirty feet. The same year, British physicist Anthony Wooldridge photographed a set of footprints and a "creature" that some experts believed to be a Yeti. Wooldridge later proved that the "creature" was a rock, but the footprints remain a mystery.

At first, it was believed that the Yeti lived in a very small area of the Himalayas. However, Yeti-like creatures have also been sighted in China and the Soviet Union. The Yeti seems to be smaller than the Bigfoot, and it apparently walks on four legs as well as on two legs. Some researchers believe that the Yeti and the Bigfoot are related; others think they may be two different creatures.

THE ALMAS

ANNA STOOD IN the doorway and looked back at her mother. "I'm going."

"Hmm. That's nice, dear."

Anna's mother was bent over the old wooden desk, studying her notebooks as if they were the most important things in the world. She called it scientific research. Anna called it boring.

"I said, I'm going, Mother."

"Yes, dear. I heard you. Be home for supper."

Anna whirled in the doorway and stomped down the stone path toward the road. What a horrible vacation! She was stuck in the mountains with nothing to do while her friends went to parties in Moscow. And all because her mother wanted to chase some silly wild man called an Almas. Why, even her mother's friends at the academy thought she was crazy.

Anna stopped at the end of the path and looked up the road toward the village. It was an easy walk—less than a kilometer. But what was the point? There was nothing to do in the village anyway. The children stared at her as if she were from another world, just because she wore city clothes. Why, they didn't even speak Russian!

She decided to walk away from the village, toward the thick forest that covered the mountainside. It was beautiful in the woods—cool and dark and secret. She had brought some bread and a piece of chicken in her knapsack. Perhaps she would have a picnic.

After three-quarters of an hour, Anna came to a rushing stream that ran into the heart of the woods. She knelt down and took a long drink of the cool water. Leaving the road, she followed the stream through the towering green trees. She hopped from rock to rock over the water, pretending she was a creature of the forest.

After a while, the forest opened onto a small clearing full of tall golden sunflowers. Anna was delighted. Such big, beautiful flowers! It was the perfect place for a picnic. She set her knapsack on a patch of grass and took out the bread and chicken. As she chewed her food, she looked around at the tall stems of the sunflowers. It was like being in a tiny forest all her own. A forest of flowers!

Something moved beyond the flowers. A shape—an animal! Anna held her breath in fear. What could it be? A bear? A wolf? No—something human. A human face staring at her through the tall green stems of the sunflowers. It was a girl!

"Hello," said Anna cautiously. "Do you speak Russian?"

The girl made a strange, whimpering sound. It was not like any language Anna had ever heard. *These mountain people!*

"My name is Anna. What's your name?"

The girl continued to stare through the green stems. *She certainly is ugly,* thought Anna. Her forehead stuck out above her eyebrows, and her nose was pressed back against her face. Her hair was long and stringy. And she hardly had any chin at all.

"Would you like some bread? Or a bite of chicken?" Anna held the food toward the strange girl.

Then she stood up and disappeared into the sunflowers.

The girl emerged from her hiding place and snatched the chicken out of Anna's hand. She took a huge bite and chewed loudly, the muscles of her jaws protruding from the sides of her face. Anna could hear the cracking of small chicken bones.

Anna was so surprised by the sudden movement and the fierce chewing that it took her a moment to realize the girl was naked. From a distance, the red hair covering her thick, muscular body almost looked like clothing. Although the strange girl was smaller than Anna, she looked strong enough to tear her to pieces. She was almost like an animal. But she wasn't an animal. Was she?

When the girl had finished the chicken, Anna handed her the piece of bread. "Poor thing, you must be starving!"

The strange girl ate the bread and held out her hand for more. Her upturned palm was hairless and wrinkled and dark. Her face was dark, too—as if she had spent her life in the sun.

"I'm sorry," said Anna. "I don't have any more food."

The girl continued to hold her wrinkled palm out toward Anna. "I'm sorry," Anna repeated.

Baring huge white teeth, the strange girl snarled like a wild dog.

Anna jumped to her feet and ran through the sunflowers toward the edge of the forest. When she reached the trees, she remembered her knapsack. It was expensive; her mother had bought it at one of the best stores in Moscow. Cautiously, Anna worked her way back through the tall flowers. The strange girl was holding the knapsack and whimpering with that pitiful sound.

"It's empty," said Anna. "But if you give it to me, I will fill it with food and come back tomorrow." She approached the girl hesitantly and took the knapsack from her wrinkled hands. "Tomorrow," she repeated. "I will see you tomorrow."

The next day Anna packed chicken, sausage, bread, and cheese and returned to the forest. The strange girl was waiting in the sunflowers, just where Anna had left her. Anna sat beside her and opened the knapsack, handing her the food piece by piece. When it was gone, the girl held out her wrinkled palm for more. This time there was no snarl.

"Tomorrow," said Anna.

With a tiny whimper, the girl brought her hand back toward her body. Then she stood up and disappeared into the sunflowers. Her light, quick movements caught Anna by surprise. As quickly as she had disappeared, the girl returned to the patch of grass. Once again she extended her wrinkled palm. There were three small red berries in the center of her hand.

Anna took the berries and held them in the sunlight. They looked harmless enough. She took a small bite and then popped them all in her mouth. They were delicious.

"Thank you," she said.

The strange girl stretched her thick lips back over her huge white teeth. It was almost like a smile.

"You must have a name," said Anna. "Everyone has a name. I know—I'll call you Sunflower. Tomorrow, Sunflower. I will see you again tomorrow."

And so it went throughout the summer. Each day Anna returned to the forest, bringing food for Sunflower. And each day Sunflower brought small gifts of her own—acorns, berries, leaves. Once she even brought a dead field mouse. It was disgusting, but Anna tried to be polite. After all, they were friends.

All too soon the time came for Anna and her mother to return to Moscow. As they packed their belongings, Anna worried about Sunflower. How would she survive? Would she live on mice and acorns?

"Are you ready, Anna?"

"Yes, Mother."

"Good. Tell me, dear, did you enjoy your vacation?"

"Oh yes, Mother, it was wonderful!"

"I'm so glad. I was afraid you would be lonely here."

"Oh, not at all. The forest is so beautiful." For a moment, Anna considered telling her mother about Sunflower. Perhaps they could take her with them to Moscow. But no, that would never do. Sunflower didn't belong in Moscow. She belonged in the sunflower forest.

"Tell me, Mother, did you enjoy *your* vacation?"

Anna's mother laughed. "Why yes, dear. I did. Of course, these mountain people can be difficult with strangers, but I think I have enough eyewitness reports to construct a picture of the Almas. I've even done a preliminary sketch. Would you like to see it?"

"Yes, please."

Anna's mother opened her briefcase and removed a sheet of rough

sketching paper. Anna took the paper from her outstretched hand and glanced at the image. Then she looked again. And again. It was just a quick sketch in pencil, but it was almost a perfect likeness. The stringy hair. The protruding forehead. The flattened nose. The receding chin. Even the short red body hair. It was Sunflower. It was her friend—the Almas.

———

Strange humanlike creatures have been observed in the mountains of Mongolia, China, and the Soviet Union for many hundreds of years. The native people of these regions call the creatures by many different names. However, most researchers use the Mongolian term, Almas. No one knows exactly what it means, but it might be translated as "wild man."

During the first half of the twentieth century, a number of Russian and Mongolian scientists studied the Almas in Mongolia. Some of their research was lost; some was hidden by the government because it feared embarrassment in the scientific world. In 1958 the Soviet Academy of Sciences established the "Snowman Commission" to study reports of humanlike creatures living in the high mountains. An expedition to the rugged Pamir Mountains of the south-central Soviet Union found interesting stories but no definite proof.

A scientist who took part in the Pamir expedition, Dr. Marie-Jeanne Koffmann, then began studying the Almas in the Caucasus Mountains of the southwestern Soviet Union. Unlike most regions where the Almas has been spotted, the Caucasus has a large human population. By 1966 Dr. Koffmann had gathered over 300 eyewitness reports. From these reports, she was able to describe a "typical" Almas. Dr. Koffmann's description, along with other details from her reports, forms the basis of this story.

Early researchers considered the Almas and the Yeti to be different names for the same creature. They called it the wild man, the Missing Link, or the Abominable Snowman. It now seems that there are at least two very different species of

"Snowman." The Yeti (and its cousin the Bigfoot) is usually described as a huge apelike creature. The Almas is usually described as a smaller and more primitive form of human being.

Some scientists believe that the Almas is a surviving Neanderthal man. According to this theory, as modern man developed and used more land, Neanderthal man was pushed higher and higher into the mountains. It is interesting that the main areas of Almas sightings are near places where Neanderthal tools and skeletons have been found. Now that communication is growing between the Soviet Union and the United States, perhaps someday soon we will know the true story of the Almas.

THE LOCH NESS MONSTER

ROBBIE MACGREGOR held his binoculars and studied the dark, churning waters of Loch Ness. About 500 yards from the shore, three cormorants bobbed up and down in the choppy waves. A casual observer might have thought they were three humps of the monster, but Robbie could see their separate bodies and the outline of their wings. His binoculars were powerful, and besides, he was no casual observer. He was an investigator.

Robbie passed over the birds and scanned the width of the loch toward Urquhart Castle, looming on the opposite shore. It was the middle of July, but a cold wind was blowing in from the North Sea. Nothing but waves and more waves. It was a bad day for Nessie. Most of the sightings took place on clear, warm summer days when the water was smooth as glass. Today, the loch looked more like a mixing bowl.

He continued scanning the waves toward the northeast. An object floated just above the waterline, but it was too big for Nessie. Probably a trawler. He angled the glasses upward and studied the sky. Storm clouds were gathering over Inverness.

"If I had any sense, I'd go home," he mumbled.

Robbie let the binoculars dangle while he checked his camera. It was equipped with a telephoto lens and high-speed film. If Nessie showed, he wanted a good, clear shot of her. That was the only way to really prove she exists—once and for all. He adjusted the focus ring on the lens. Then he raised his binoculars and scanned the loch again.

Like most Highlanders, Robbie had heard stories of Nessie for as long as he could remember. He had spent hours looking into the deep, murky waters of Loch Ness, waiting patiently for the creature to appear. But he had never seen her. Finally, he had convinced his parents to let him camp out on the beach. After all, he was sixteen now, and the real investigators spent days, even weeks, camped along the shore.

Robbie glanced again at the clouds over Inverness. Of course the real investigators had nice dry vans or trailers to protect them from the weather. He looked back across the narrow, rocky beach to his pup tent; it was better than nothing. And the cliffs would provide some protection. The main thing was to keep the camera dry. He reached into the pocket of his mackintosh, pulled out a plastic bag, and slipped it over the long telephoto lens.

In the early evening, it began to drizzle. Robbie stood on the rocky shore, scanning the loch through the fine, gray rain. The light was still good. But as the rain grew harder, the sky darkened, and the churning waters of the loch turned black as pitch.

"Achhh! I couldn't tell Nessie from a log in this weather." With a sigh of disappointment, Robbie crossed the beach and crawled into his tent.

The heart of the storm arrived around midnight. The rain pounded on the sides of the tent, and the wind howled through the flaps. Robbie lay awake, listening to the sounds of the storm and thinking of the deep black waters of the loch. "Where are you, Nessie?" he asked aloud. "Do you like the rain?"

A black hump emerged from the foam. . . . It was Nessie!

Sometime in the early morning, Robbie fell into a dreamless sleep. He was awakened by the sound of a cormorant, cawing loudly as it hunted for fish. Robbie opened his eyes slowly and stared at the roof of the tent. Except for the noisy bird, everything was quiet. Quiet! The rain was over!

He crawled from the tent and gazed out over the loch. The rising sun was shining on the hills near Urquhart Castle. The wind and clouds were gone. The water was smooth as glass.

Robbie caught a sudden flash of movement a hundred yards from the shore. The water began to bubble and boil with thick foam. Robbie ran across the beach to the edge of the loch. A black hump emerged from the foam. It looked like an overturned boat. But it wasn't a boat. It was Nessie!

He reached down for his binoculars. "Achhh!" They were still in the tent. The camera, too.

Out in the water, the hump was growing and growing. It was huge! Now a smaller hump appeared in front of the big one; it was growing, too, curving upward. No, it wasn't a hump at all. It was her neck. And her head. Nessie was looking at him!

Robbie gazed in wonder at the huge hump, the long neck, the tiny head—all black and glistening in the rising sun. "Hello, Nessie," he whispered. "Stay right where you are."

Very slowly he began to back up over the narrow beach, keeping Nessie in his sight. "One picture," he pleaded. "Just one good picture." He was almost at the tent now, and she was still posing motionless in the water. The camera was in the plastic bag, tucked in his pack in the back of the tent. It would take ten seconds—maybe less. He knelt down on the rocks. Then he scrambled into the tent, grabbed the camera, and scrambled back onto the beach. He stared at the loch in disbelief. Nessie was gone.

"Achhh!" Robbie moaned. He walked back down to the shore and examined the surface of the loch. A circle of waves remained where Nessie had

disappeared. The waves spread outward and outward, finally lapping at the rocks beneath his feet.

For a long time, Robbie scanned the loch for signs of Nessie. But there was nothing. He had seen her. And she was gone—back to her home in the cold, deep water.

Finally, he tore down his tent and packed away his binoculars and his camera with the telephoto lens. The investigation was over—at least for now.

Before he left, Robbie stood one last time on the rocky shore and looked out over the dark, waveless loch. A slight smile crept over his face. "Good-bye, Nessie," he said. "I'll see you again."

———

Loch Ness is a deep, dark lake in the Highlands of Scotland. For centuries, the people who live near the loch have told stories of a strange beast living in the

murky waters. However, 1933 was the year that made Nessie famous. Over ninety people claimed to have seen the monster that year, and many of these stories were published in newspapers throughout the world. The sightings increased in 1934, with over 130 reports. A new road was built along the loch during these years, bringing more people to the area and allowing a better view of the water. Also, it's believed the dynamite used in building the road may have brought Nessie to the surface.

Today, over 4,000 people have claimed to have seen the Loch Ness Monster. Some of these reports were hoaxes, and others were sightings of normal objects or animals mistaken in the distance. But there still remain hundreds of sightings by reliable witnesses.

The general picture of Nessie from these reports is of a dark creature twenty to forty feet long, with at least one hump rising above the water, a long, thin neck, and a small head. Although most sightings take place in the water, a few people say they have seen Nessie on the land.

There have been many photographs of the creature, but none are clear enough to provide absolute proof that it exists. A film taken by Tim Dinsdale in 1960 is one of the strongest pieces of evidence. It shows an object moving through the water without the kind of waves that would be created by a boat. The film was analyzed by British military intelligence experts in 1966. They concluded that it was probably an animal at least six feet wide, five feet high, and twelve to sixteen feet long.

Since the mid-1960s, investigators have used sophisticated technology to look for Nessie. In 1968 sonar readings by scientists from the University of Birmingham indicated that there was a group of large animals in the loch, diving to great depths at surprising speeds. An underwater photograph taken in 1972 appears to show a large flipper; another photograph taken in 1975 seems to show the outline of a long-necked beast with a large body and two fins. Divers and mini-

submarines have also searched for Nessie, but they have been hampered by the poor visibility in the murky water.

Early researchers imagined Nessie to be a single creature that had wandered into Loch Ness from the sea. It is now clear that, if Nessie exists, there must be a whole population of large, unknown animals living and breeding in Loch Ness. The question is, what are they? Researchers have considered different types of creatures: 1) a long-necked aquatic mammal related to a seal or manatee; 2) a long, thin whale similar to the zeuglodon, thought to have become extinct 25 million years ago; 3) an aquatic reptile similar to the plesiosaur, thought to have become extinct 65 million years ago; 4) an amphibian similar to a giant salamander or newt; 5) a giant eel; or 6) an invertebrate similar to a giant worm or sea slug.

Nessie is only one of many strange creatures that have been reported living in cold, deep lakes in the Northern Hemisphere. Other famous lake monsters include Ogapogo, in Lake Okanagan, located in British Columbia, and Champie, in Lake Champlain, located in upper New York State. Monsters have been reported in other Scottish lakes, as well as in Ireland, Sweden, and the Soviet Union. These creatures may all be the same type of animal, but the evidence suggests that there may be more than one kind of unknown animal living in the cold lakes of the north.

THE LUSCA

B ENJAMIN PUSHED OFF from the rocky shore and sculled with one of the long wooden oars. As he disturbed the crystal-clear water, a school of tiny, iridescent fish scattered into a maze of pink coral. Benjamin smiled. *Grow big,* he thought. *Perhaps we will meet again.*

When the dinghy was free of the underwater rocks, Benjamin set the oars in place and pulled away from the island. In the bow, his older brother, Caleb, gazed out over the clear blue water. "Pull, Benjamin," said Caleb. "The fish are waiting."

"I'm pulling," said Benjamin. It was early morning, but the sun was already hot, and he could feel salty sweat dripping into his eyes.

"Do you want me to do it?" asked Caleb.

"No," said Benjamin, straining hard against the long wooden oars. "I can do it myself."

After an hour of hard pulling, they were beyond the reef and into the Tongue of the Ocean, the deep blue water that stretches to the east of Andros Island in the Bahamas. Caleb stood in the bow of the dinghy and surveyed the surface with the practiced eye of an expert. Finally, he pointed to an indigo-blue patch of water. "There," he said. "I can feel the fish."

Like a vicious whip, a giant tentacle broke the surface . . .

Benjamin rowed quickly toward the dark blue patch. Sometimes it was difficult to be Caleb's brother, but to fish with him was an honor. When Caleb could feel the fish, the catch would be big.

"All right," said Caleb. "Now scull gently while I let out the line."

Benjamin worked the oars easily through the water, trying to keep the boat steady as Caleb let the huge coil of line run through his hands. When the line was out, Caleb began to bring it up, slowly and steadily. Benjamin smiled in admiration of his brother's strong, sure movements. The tourists used big powerboats and thick poles with metal reels, but Caleb needed nothing but a dinghy and a handline. That, and a good partner to keep the boat steady.

When the line was halfway into the boat, Caleb's face grew strained; he began to breathe heavily.

"What's wrong?" asked Benjamin.

"The line's stuck. It must be caught on the bottom."

"What should I do?"

"Row in a circle—very slowly."

Benjamin did as he was told. In the bow of the dinghy, Caleb strained on the handline, trying to loosen it from the bottom. Sweat ran down his face, and the muscles in his arms seemed ready to explode. Finally, with one great effort, the line began to move.

"Is it loose?" asked Benjamin.

"It's off the bottom," said Caleb, still straining on the handline. "But it's caught on something . . . very . . . heavy."

"Maybe it's a big fish."

"No, the big fish fight . . . or move. This is just hanging on the line."

"Maybe it's treasure!"

Caleb smiled slightly as he continued to pull the handline into the dinghy. "We'll know . . . soon enough."

When most of the line was coiled in the bow, Caleb leaned over slightly and looked down.

"What is it?" asked Benjamin.

Caleb continued to stare into the water, pulling on the handline. Suddenly his face contorted in horror. "No!"

Like a vicious whip, a giant tentacle broke the surface and wrapped around Caleb's body. Another tentacle exploded on the side of the boat and circled the dinghy as if it were a toy. "Help!" cried Caleb. "The Lusca!"

Benjamin grabbed a wooden oar and pounded the rubbery mass of flesh that stretched across the dinghy separating him from Caleb. The tentacle was as thick as a man's body; the huge suckers held the boat like a powerful adhesive. The Lusca was pulling the dinghy downward into the Tongue of the Ocean. Then suddenly the giant arm arched high in the air and disappeared into the sea. Benjamin looked desperately toward the bow of the dinghy. Caleb was gone!

Rushing to the front of the boat, Benjamin peered down into the water. The Lusca writhed directly below him—a huge bulbous head and eight grotesque arms that stretched as far as he could see—one arm still coiled tightly around Caleb.

Caleb was struggling fiercely. But he couldn't hold out for long underwater.

Benjamin grabbed a fish knife and dove into the water, swimming down toward Caleb. After what seemed like hours, he reached his brother. Benjamin hacked at the rubbery tentacle—it was useless. The creature's flesh was hard and thick; the giant suckers held Caleb imprisoned in their deadly grasp.

Lungs ready to burst, Benjamin swam toward the monstrous head. Now he was face to face with the Lusca. Its eyes were like great saucers, looking back at him with a strange, horrible intelligence. Benjamin tightened his

grip on the fish knife and drove the blade deep into the eye of the Lusca.

The sea was filled with inky blackness. Benjamin fought through the dark water toward Caleb, groping desperately for his brother's body. His lungs were burning, and his head was spinning, but that didn't matter. It was Caleb that mattered. He had to find Caleb.

He brushed against something in the darkness. Soft flesh. Human flesh. Caleb—floating freely in the inky water. The Lusca was gone.

Breaking the surface, Benjamin gasped for air, filling his lungs again and again. Then he boosted Caleb into the dinghy and struggled in after him. He laid his palms against his brother's chest and pushed. Water spurted out of Caleb's lungs, and Benjamin blew breath back into his body. Again and again, Benjamin pressed and blew, pressed and blew, until Caleb began to breathe on his own. After a few shallow breaths, Caleb's eyes fluttered open. He was alive.

"How do you feel?" asked Benjamin.

Caleb smiled weakly. "Thank you," he said.

"Is anything broken?"

"I don't think so. But my back hurts."

"Let me see." Carefully Benjamin rolled his brother over. Caleb yelped with pain. In the center of his back was a large round wound where the skin had been torn away, exposing the bloody red tissue underneath. It was a perfect circle—the size of a sucker on the monster's arm. It was the mark of the Lusca.

Sailors have told stories of sea monsters for as long as man has sailed the sea. One of the most famous monsters was the Kraken, a huge, many-armed creature reported by Norwegian sailors in the north Atlantic. For hundreds of years, most people considered the Kraken to be a fantasy animal. Then, in the 1870s, animals very similar to the Kraken began to wash up on the beaches of Newfoundland—across the Atlantic from Norway. Upon examining these creatures, scientists discovered that they were giant squid. The largest known specimen of giant squid is around sixty feet long, but some experts believe there may be specimens twice that size.

Although the giant squid probably explains the tales of the Kraken, the Lusca is another story. The Lusca is a many-armed monster—half octopus, half dragon—reported by natives of Andros Island in the Bahamas. It is said to live in inland lakes and water-filled holes, as well as in the depths of the ocean. Just as most scientists once believed that the Kraken was a myth, many believe that the Lusca is a creature of fantasy. Others think the Lusca is a giant squid. Some scientists and fishermen, however, believe that the Lusca is really a giant octopus.

Unlike the giant squid, the giant octopus has not yet been officially accepted by the scientific world. But there is strong evidence that the giant octopus does exist

and that it may be even larger than the giant squid—perhaps as long as 200 feet from tentacle tip to tentacle tip! It's difficult to estimate the weight of such a creature, but it would certainly weigh many tons. (The largest known octopus measures about twenty feet from tip to tip and weighs around 125 pounds.)

The strongest evidence for the existence of the giant octopus is a carcass that washed up on the beach of St. Augustine, Florida, in 1896. Although the carcass was partially decayed, those who examined it believed that it was the remains of a huge octopus. Pieces of arms were found buried in the sand nearby; the longest measured over thirty-two feet. Based on the size of the carcass and the partial arms, the octopus would have had arms seventy-five to one hundred feet long, thus measuring between 150 and 200 feet from tip to tip. The carcass alone—without the arms—was estimated to weigh six tons.

In 1897 Professor A. E. Verrill, a highly respected expert on cephalopods—animals like the octopus and squid—agreed that the Florida sea monster was probably an octopus. After studying photographs and tissue samples, Dr. Verrill gave it the scientific name Octopus giganteus, which means "giant octopus." However, Dr. Verrill later changed his mind, without ever examining the carcass. Fortunately, a sample of the carcass was preserved at the Smithsonian Institution. Over seventy years later, a team of scientists discovered this sample and tested it using modern laboratory techniques. These tests indicate that the Florida sea monster was more similar to the octopus than to any other known animal.

The giant squid and giant octopus may explain many-armed sea monsters like the Kraken and the Lusca. However, most reports of sea monsters describe long necks or snakelike bodies. These are often called sea serpents. The zoologist Bernard Heuvelmans has studied almost 600 reports of sea serpents over the centuries. He believes these reports may be based on at least seven different unknown animals. Science has solved the mystery of the Kraken by discovering the giant squid, and the mystery of the Lusca may be solved with the discovery of the giant octopus. Perhaps some day the mystery of the sea serpents may be solved as well.

THE MOKELE-MBEMBE

DAHKA STALKED THROUGH the dark forest in the way of the great Pygmy hunters. His eyes missed nothing; his ears were tuned to the slightest sound. For years he had watched his father and the other men of the band. Now it was his turn to bring home the evening meal.

Dahka turned toward a rustling in the rotting leaves and watched a python slither across the muddy floor of the forest. His heart beat quickly with excitement. He had been hunting since early morning, and this was the biggest animal he had seen. *It is a good python*, he thought. *It will make many meals.*

The boy reached into his quiver and withdrew a poisoned arrow. In one smooth motion, he placed the arrow into his crossbow, pulled back on the string, and aimed at the vulnerable spot between the eyes of the snake. Before he could release the arrow, a monkey screeched loudly in the trees, warning the other monkeys that the deadly python was approaching.

"Hoo hoo hoo hoo! Hoo hoo hoo hoo!"

For a moment, Dahka took his eyes off the snake and turned toward the

noisy monkey. When he looked back at the ground, the python had disappeared into the thick green vegetation.

"Stupid monkey," he muttered angrily. "Come down where I can see you, and I'll take *you* home for supper."

Dahka continued onward, pushing and hacking his way through the thick vegetation. Although it was the dry season, his feet sank into the muddy ooze. Occasionally, he would step into a puddle and sink up to his knees. The Likouala swamps were not an easy place to walk. But they made an excellent place to hunt.

In the early afternoon, Dahka broke through the edge of the swampy forest and stood on the shore of Lake Telle. After the dense forest, the broad, flat lake seemed enormous. Dahka could barely see the opposite shore.

Holding his crossbow above his head, Dahka waded out into the dark water. The lake was very shallow, and even a Pygmy could walk near the shore. It was easier than walking through the forest, and there were plenty of crocodiles and turtles to hunt.

Near the shore, perhaps a kilometer away, Dahka noticed a disturbance in the smooth surface of the lake. Something was emerging from the water. It looked like a snake, but a snake cannot stand up straight in the water. Dahka gazed across the surface. *What is it?* he wondered. *It's not a fish or a crocodile, and it's too big to be a turtle. Maybe it's the trunk of an elephant!* If he killed an elephant, he would be a great hunter. The whole band would have a feast!

Dahka waded toward the animal, quickly yet silently. He passed crocodiles and turtles swimming in the shallow water, but he was not interested in them. *What hunter would want a turtle if he could have an elephant?*

As Dahka drew closer, the elephant's trunk looked stranger and stranger.

Dahka stared in horror as a huge dark shape emerged from the molibo.

There seemed to be a huge eye and a small head at the end, but he was still too far away to see clearly. Perhaps it was just the angle. Or a trick of the light. He would know soon enough.

When Dahka was within a few hundred meters of the animal, the trunk began to move toward a muddy stream—a *molibo*—flowing into the lake. Dahka waded desperately toward the mouth of the stream. He had to catch the elephant before it disappeared into the forest. He reached the mouth and began to wade upstream through the murky water of the molibo. Soon he was surrounded by the dark forest. The water was up to his chest, and thick patches of floating grass grabbed his arms like water snakes.

Panting with exhaustion, Dahka stopped and gazed up the molibo into the dense forest. There was no sign of the elephant. If it had left the water, he would have heard it and seen tracks on the shore. No, it was still in the molibo. *But where is it?* he wondered. *Elephants do not disappear.*

Suddenly, the water exploded around him. Dahka stared in horror as a huge dark shape emerged from the molibo. It grew larger and larger until it was bigger than an elephant—bigger than two elephants or three elephants! Its massive body glistened in the sun. Its powerful tail was like a great tree floating on the surface of the molibo. It had a neck like a python, a head like a giant turtle, and cold crocodile eyes that stared down at Dahka as if he were nothing more than a piece of floating grass.

No, it was not an elephant. It was the monster of the swamps. Mokele-Mbembe.

Dahka stared wide-eyed at the huge beast towering above him and gripped his crossbow tightly in his hands. His heart was beating louder than a thousand drums, but his hunter's instinct took control. He reached for a poisoned arrow, set it into the crossbow, and pulled back on the string.

Like a flash of lightning, Mokele-Mbembe's powerful tail whipped across the water and smashed Dahka into the molibo. The boy struggled

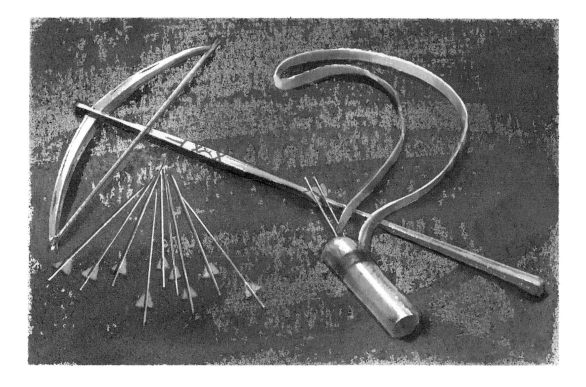

in the floating grass, gasping for breath as he tried to regain his footing. His crossbow was gone. He was at the mercy of the monster.

Back on his feet, Dahka found himself staring directly into the cold eyes of Mokele-Mbembe. For a moment, the beast seemed to contemplate whether the boy might make a good meal. Then the monster turned its heavy body and waded toward the shore. Dahka watched as Mokele-Mbembe stopped to eat the molombo fruit that grew along the edge of the stream. When it had eaten its fill, the great beast stepped out of the water and smashed its way through the trees.

After Mokele-Mbembe was gone, Dahka searched for his crossbow in the muddy bottom of the molibo. When he found it, he waded across the stream and climbed onto the bank. He breathed deeply and tried to steady his heart.

The path of the monster was like an open road through the swamps—

wide enough for two elephants to walk side by side. Dahka followed the path for a few steps; then he walked into the darkness of the forest. It was late, and he was empty-handed. Perhaps he would find that python. If not, maybe the monkey.

Huge monsters that look like dinosaurs have been reported by the natives of tropical Africa for at least 200 years. The description of these creatures is similar to that of a sauropod, a plant-eating dinosaur with a massive body, powerful tail, long neck, and small head. The sauropods were the largest animals ever to live on land. One type of sauropod, Diplodocus, was eighty-two feet long; another type, Brachiosaurus, weighed fifty tons. However, the sauropods reported from Africa are probably much smaller than these extremes.

The modern search for living sauropods began in the late 1970s. A scientist named James Powell showed pictures of various animals to the native people of Gabon, located along the equator in central Africa. When he showed them a picture of a sauropod, they identified it as "N'yamala" and said that it lived in remote jungle lakes. Powell reported his findings to another scientist named Roy Mackal, and together they planned an expedition to search for the N'yamala.

After studying the historical reports, Powell and Mackal concluded that the N'yamala was the same animal as the Mokele-Mbembe, a sauropodlike creature described by the people of the Congo, located east of Gabon. The scientists also concluded that the best place to look for Mokele-Mbembe would be the Likouala swamps in the northeastern part of the Congo. In 1980, Powell and Mackal went to the Likouala region and interviewed the Pygmies and Bantus who live near the swamps. The next year, Mackal returned with a second expedition. Although these expeditions found no definite proof, they obtained many additional reports from native people.

At the same time that the second Mackal expedition was exploring the rivers

of the Likouala region, another American expedition, led by an engineer named Herman Regusters, reached Lake Telle in the heart of the swamps. Regusters claimed to have photographed Mokele-Mbembe in the lake. However, the photographs were not clear, and other information provided by Regusters was confusing.

In 1983 a new expedition was led by a Congolese zoologist, Marcellin Agnagna. Agnagna claimed to have seen Mokele-Mbembe in Lake Telle. As a trained zoologist, Agnagna was familiar with the animals that live in the Likouala swamps, and he was unlikely to mistake one animal for another. He described Mokele-Mbembe as a reptile approximately sixteen feet long above the water, with a broad black back, a long neck, a small head, and oval crocodilian eyes. He drew a sketch that looks very similar to a sauropod.

Since 1983 there have been at least three additional expeditions to the Likouala swamps, one British group and two Japanese groups. None of these expeditions has seen Mokele-Mbembe. The second Japanese group reported that the creature probably does not actually live in Lake Telle, but rather in the molibos, small jungle streams that flow into the lake.

Is there a living dinosaur in the swamps of the Congo? To the native people, Mokele-Mbembe is as real as the elephant or the monkey. Herman Regusters and Marcellin Agnagna claim to have seen it. Scientists like Roy Mackal and James Powell think it is very possible. The tropical swamps of central Africa were never covered with ice during the Ice Ages, and they have changed relatively little since the days of the dinosaurs, over 65 million years ago. Mokele-Mbembe may be waiting for the next expedition.

THE KONGAMATO

THE JIUNDU RIVER snaked its way through the thick green swamp. As the hunting party approached the bank, Mbula held up his hand, and the porters came to a stop. The white hunter wiped the sweat from his forehead and turned toward the African boy.

"What's wrong?" asked the hunter.

"The river," said Mbula.

"I can see the blasted river," said the hunter. "Is it deep?"

"No, sir," said Mbula. "Very shallow."

"Well, let's cross it."

Mbula glanced politely away from the older man. "Soon, sir. Very soon."

Reaching into his bag, Mbula removed the mulendi root and the cup made of bark. Then, squatting on the soft, swampy ground, he began to cut the root into strips with his sharp knife.

"What in blazes are you doing?" asked the hunter.

"*Muchi wa Kongamato,*" said Mbula quietly.

"Speak English, boy."

"It is a protection."

"A protection? Against what?"

Out of the sky, a huge red monster swooped toward the hunter . . .

Mbula's voice dropped to a whisper: "Kongamato."

"What in blazes is Kongamato?"

"Please, sir," Mbula begged. "It is better that we do not speak of it."

When the mulendi root had been cut into narrow strips, Mbula took a piece of vine from his bag and tied half of the strips into a small bundle. Then he set the remaining strips on a flat rock and began to grind them with the back of his knife. The white hunter stood above him impatiently, staring angrily at the river and wiping the sweat from his forehead. Forming a small circle around them, the porters watched in deadly seriousness.

"This is ridiculous," said the hunter finally. "I'm not going to stand and wait for this blasted native witchcraft. If you're afraid of Kongawhatcha-callit, that's fine. I'm crossing the river." Breaking through the circle, the hunter headed for the muddy Jiundu.

"Please, sir," cried Mbula. "Wait for protection!" Acting quickly, the boy scooped the powdered root into the cup. Then he poured a bit of water from his canteen onto the powder until it became a thin, watery paste. When the mixture was ready, he rose to his feet and ran after the white hunter. "Please, sir! Wait!"

The hunter was already halfway into the river, up to his waist in the muddy water, holding his rifle high above his head. Just as Mbula reached the bank, a great wind whipped the water and shook the tops of the trees.

Out of the sky, a huge red monster swooped toward the white hunter. Its wings were half as wide as the river. Knife-sharp teeth flashed in its long, ugly beak, and razorlike claws curled from its feet and hands. It was a bird and a lizard and a bat in one horrible nightmare. It was the Kongamato.

Running toward the hunter, Mbula dipped his bundle of root strips into the cup and sprinkled the paste onto the surface of the water. *"Muchi wa Kongamato,"* he chanted. *"Muchi wa Kongamato."*

Out in the water, the hunter turned toward the flying monster and raised

his rifle. He was too late. The Kongamato swooped down and knocked the gun from his hands as if it were a twig. The hunter tumbled into the muddy water of the Jiundu, his arms and legs flailing like a madman's.

A moment later, Mbula reached the center of the river and pulled the hunter to the surface. He had swallowed water, but there were no cuts or bruises. Slinging the man's arm over his shoulder, the boy helped him back to the shore. He made him comfortable on the swampy ground and poured cool, clean water over his face. The hunter was still breathing heavily, and his eyes were glazed with terror. But he would recover.

"You are very brave, sir," said Mbula soothingly. "Few white men have seen the swamp of the Jiundu. But you are foolish, too. Next time you will wait for protection."

Looking toward the muddy water of the river, Mbula whispered very quietly, "*Muchi wa Kongamato.*"

This story is based on a tradition of the Kaonde, a tribe that lives in northwestern Zambia. The mulendi root paste is a charm used at river crossings for protection against the Kongamato, as reported by a British official named Frank H. Melland. When Melland asked the Kaonde to describe the Kongamato, they at first said it was like a bird. Then they said it was more like a lizard with wings like a bat's. Finally, Melland showed them pictures of various animals, including a prehistoric flying reptile called a pterodactyl. The Kaonde said the pterodactyl looked just like the Kongamato.

Strange flying monsters have been sighted in other areas of Africa, as well as in America and Asia. In the first half of the twentieth century, a sixteen-year-old boy in Namibia claimed to have seen a giant flying snake, and missionaries in Kenya reported "flying dragons." More recent expeditions obtained accounts of flying creatures resembling pterosaurs in both these areas. (Pterosaur is a general term for prehistoric flying reptiles, including the pterodactyl.) In the 1980s there were even reports of pterosaurlike creatures in southern Texas.

In 1932 zoologist Ivan Sanderson was wading across a river in Cameroon, located to the northwest of Zambia, when he was attacked by a horrible black creature with sharp teeth and wings at least twelve feet wide. The native people told him that this was an "Olitiau," and they begged him to leave the area at once. Some researchers believe that the Olitiau and the Kongamato may both be pterosaurs. However, Dr. Sanderson thought the Olitiau was actually a giant carnivorous bat—much larger than any bat known to science. A similar batlike monster called the Ahool has been described by native people on the island of Java in Indonesia.

If the Olitiau and the Ahool are proven to be huge bats, it would be an important scientific discovery. But if the Kongamato is proven to be a living pterosaur, it would be a true scientific breakthrough. The pterosaurs, along with the other

dinosaurs, are believed to have died out over 65 million years ago. Could they still exist in the Jiundu swamp of Zambia? Some experts think it is very possible. The Jiundu swamp is similar to the Likouala swamps of the Congo, where Mokele-Mbembe has been sighted (see page 42). Like Mokele-Mbembe, the Kongamato may be a living dinosaur.

Annotated Bibliography

Dinsdale, Tim. *Monster Hunt*. Washington D.C.: Acropolis Books, Ltd., 1972. Originally published as *The Leviathans*, 1966. Dinsdale was one of the most dedicated Loch Ness researchers; contains good illustrations, including stills from his famous film.

Gould, Rupert T. *The Loch Ness Monster and Others*. New York: University Books, 1969. Originally published by Geoffrey Bles, London, 1934. The first serious investigation of the Loch Ness monster; contains many early eyewitness accounts.

Green, John W. *Sasquatch: The Apes Among Us*. Seattle: Hancock House, 1978. The most comprehensive book on the Bigfoot mystery.

Heuvelmans, Bernard. *On the Track of Unknown Animals*. Tr. by Richard Garnett. New York: Hill and Wang, 1959. The classic work by the father of cryptozoology; contains information on all the animals in this book, as well as many others.

International Society of Cryptozoology. *Cryptozoology*. Volumes 1–8, 1982–1989. A scholarly journal published annually; contains research papers, field reports, and laboratory analysis; the best source for current information on cryptozoology.

———. *ISC Newsletter*. 1982–1990. A quarterly newsletter containing up-to-date reports on current research.

Mackal, Roy P. *The Monsters of Loch Ness*. Chicago: The Swallow Press, 1976. A scientific study of the Loch Ness mystery by the foremost American cryptozoologist.

_____. *Searching for Hidden Animals: An Inquiry into Zoological Mysteries*. Garden City, New York: Doubleday & Company, 1980. Contains chapters on the Giant Octopus, the Kongamato, and the N'yamala (Mokele-Mbembe).

_____. *A Living Dinosaur? In Search of Mokele-Mbembe*. New York: E. J. Brill, 1987. A fascinating account of Mackal's two expeditions to the Likouala swamps.

Napier, John. *Bigfoot: The Yeti and Sasquatch in Myth and Reality*. New York: E. P. Dutton & Co., 1973. Dr. Napier was an expert on primates; in this book, he expressed belief in the possibility of the Sasquatch (Bigfoot) but was doubtful about the Yeti.

Sanderson, Ivan T. *Investigating the Unexplained: A Compendium of Disquieting Mysteries of the Natural World*. Englewood Cliffs, New Jersey: Prentice-Hall, 1972. Contains four chapters on hidden animals, including the author's personal experience with giant flying creatures.

Shackley, Myra L. *Still Living? Yeti, Sasquatch and the Neanderthal Enigma*. New York: Thames and Hudson, 1983. Contains information on the Almas, Yeti, and Sasquatch, as well as on Chinese and Siberian creatures.

Wood, F. G., and Joseph F. Gennaro, Jr. "An Octopus Trilogy." *National History*, March 1971. Describes the research and scientific analysis that led to identification of the Florida sea monster as a giant octopus.

Wright, Bruce. "The Lusca of Andros." *The Atlantic Advocate*, June 1967. Describes native reports of the Lusca on Andros Island.

Bigfoot

Lusca

Loch Ness M

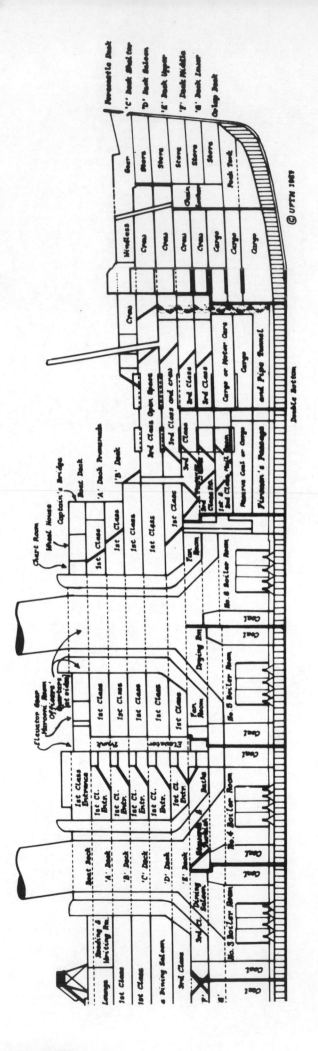